NEW DIMENSIONS OF PEACEKEEPING

AF719190

NIJHOFF LAW SPECIALS

D. Campbell, Abortion Law and Public Policy. 1984.
ISBN 90-247-3107-0

J. Pictet, Development and Principles of International Humanitarian Law. 1985.
ISBN 90-247-3199-2

J. van Houtte, Sociology of Law and Legal Anthropology in Dutch-speaking Countries. 1985.
ISBN 90-247-3175-5

C.D. De Fouloy, Glossary of NAFTA Terms. 1994.
ISBN 0-7923-2719-5

H.L. Zielinski, Health and Humanitarian Concerns. Principles and Ethics. 1994
ISBN 0-7923-2963-5

K.S. Foster and D.C. Alexander, Prospects of a US-Chile Free Trade Agreement. 1994
ISBN 0-7923-2885-X

F.J.M. Feldbrugge (ed.), Russian Federation Legislative Survey. June 1990-December 1992. 1995
ISBN 0-7923-3243-1

R. Platzöder (ed.), The 1994 United Nations Convention on the Law of the Sea. Basic Documents with an Introduction. 1995
ISBN 0-7923-3271-7

D. Warner (ed.), New Dimensions of Peacekeeping. 1995
ISBN 0-7923-3301-2

JX
1981
.7
N45
1995

New Dimensions of Peacekeeping

Edited by

Daniel Warner

MARTINUS NIJHOFF PUBLISHERS
DORDRECHT / BOSTON / LONDON

LAW LIBRARY
FEB - 6 1997
GOLDEN GATE UNIVERSITY

A C.I.P. Catalogue record for this book is available from the Library of Congress.

ISBN 0-7923-3301-2

Published by Martinus Nijhoff Publishers,
P.O. Box 163, 3300 AD Dordrecht, The Netherlands.

Sold and distributed in the U.S.A. and Canada
by Kluwer Academic Publishers,
101 Philip Drive, Norwell, MA 02061, U.S.A.

In all other countries, sold and distributed
by Kluwer Academic Publishers Group,
P.O. Box 322, 3300 AH Dordrecht, The Netherlands.

Printed on acid-free paper

All Rights Reserved
© 1995 Kluwer Academic Publishers
Kluwer Academic Publishers incorporates the publishing programmes of
Martinus Nijhoff Publishers.

No part of the material protected by this copyright notice may be reproduced or
utilized in any form or by any means, electronic or mechanical,
including photocopying, recording, or by any information storage and
retrieval system, without written permission from the copyright owner.

Printed in the Netherlands

TABLE OF CONTENTS

PREFACE

World attention has turned to peacekeeping operations because of the acceleration of United Nations activities in this area. The list of countries where the UN is carrying out peacekeeping operations of some sort continues to expand. In fact, it has grown at a rate that has surpassed the abilities of both the UN and scholars to grasp the implications of the ad hoc arrangements that have been put together in one crisis situation after another.

As part of a series of activities organized in celebration of the United Nations' 50th anniversary in 1995, the Graduate Institute of International Studies, with the support of the Japan Foundation, organized a Colloquium on "New Dimensions of Peacekeeping" on March 10-11, 1994, in Geneva. The purpose of the meeting was to bring together academics and practitioners to discuss the evolution of peacekeeping and to try to find certain patterns in that evolution that would anticipate future trends and needs. It was, in many ways, a unique opportunity for academics and practitioners to take stock of what has happened and what is happening in the peacekeeping arena.

The first day was devoted to public presentations and discussions. After Professor Georges Abi-Saab gave a brief overview of the issues involved in old and new UN peacekeeping, Professor Victor-Yves Ghebali, Professor Steven R. Ratner and Serge Lalande presented papers on three case studies: the Former Yugoslavia, Cambodia and Somalia. The presentations were followed by a lively debate, which is summarized, as are all the discussions, by the Rapporteur, Dr. Connie Peck, in the final section of the book. Ambassador Hisashi Owada gave the keynote address on "The Japanese Perspective on Peacekeeping," which was followed by a short question-and-answer period.

The second day involved closed sessions with invited guests. The first session focussed on substantive activities, with brief presentations by Dr. Mats Berdal on "Military Aspects of Peacekeeping," Mr. S.V. DeMello on "Humanitarian Aspects of Peacekeeping," and Dr. Ronald Dreyer on "Democracy and State-Building." Mrs. Sadako Ogata, UN High Commissioner for Refugees, gave an address on "The Interface Between Peacekeeping and Humanitarian Action."

The final session dealt with managing peacekeeping. Mr. Ralph Zacklin presented "Managing Peacekeeping from a Legal Perspective," Mr. Maurice Betrand explained "The Confusion Between Peacemaking and Peacekeeeping," and Mr. Elie Marcuse spoke on "The Former Yugoslavia: NATO's Role." The presentations in all sessions were followed by discussions among the participants.

Because the very nature of peacekeeping is constantly evolving, one is hesitant to publish the proceedings of a Colloquium of this sort because the material could quickly become out of date. On the other hand, because the subject is so important and the interest shown considerable, one puts forward the proceedings as input into the ongoing debate about the future of UN activities in this field. Indeed, the very expansion of UN activities and the world's growing attention to the missions add a more urgent dimension to the debate about new dimensions in UN peacekeeping.

We would like to express our deep appreciation to the Japan Foundation for its support, Ambassador Minoru Endo of the Japanese Mission in Geneva, and especially to Mr. Korenari Kai, Counselor in the Mission, for his enthusiastic contribution. Ms. Stephanie Kleine-Ahlbrandt and Mrs. Brenda Watson Newmann were invaluable in transferring the Colloquium papers into manuscript form.

Daniel Warner
Geneva, August 1994

INTRODUCTION

United Nations peacekeeping is faced with unprecedented challenges. The end of the Cold War has brought about an enormous upsurge in ethnic, religious and other local conflicts. Many of these conflicts pre-date the Cold War period and have deep historical and cultural roots. Because of their serious humanitarian implications or consequences for international peace and security there is no other alternative for the international community than to respond to these conflicts with a view to their resolution, or at least to their alleviation. These challenges have strained the capacity and resources of the United Nations, which had been used to more traditional, inter-state disputes and conflicts during the first forty-five years of its existence.

The 1990's have seen wide swings in public opinion towards United Nations peacekeeping. The euphoria and high expectations regarding what the United Nations can deliver have been replaced by the rude shocks and deflated assessments of its capacity to successfully cope with conflicts. In this context, it would be highly desirable that a judicious balance be struck in the evaluation of United Nations peacekeeping activities, which takes fully into account the great potential they have for contributing to international peace and security and to the reduction of human suffering. At the same time, such a review should include a candid discussion regarding the weaknesses and shortcomings of peacekeeping activities. It is therefore most timely that the Geneva Graduate Institute of International Studies brought together academics and practitioners to discuss the new dimensions of peacekeeping. It is necessary that the theory of international conflict and peacekeeping be constantly tested and enriched by the practical experience of peacekeeping operations which contain valuable lessons for the future.

It is essential that we bear in mind the benefits of classical peacekeeping, which are based on such time-honoured principles as the consent of the parties to the conflict and the willingness of the troop contributors for a United Nations presence, the non-partisan and non-combatant character of peacekeepers and the minimum use of force for the purpose of self-defence alone. Any deviation from these principles should be looked at seriously for their very far-reaching consequences.

Recent peacekeeping operations have increasingly ventured into an ambitious, multi-dimensional undertaking for "failed States", intended for building new institutions for democratic self-governance, national reconciliation and nation-building. United Nations operations in Cambodia, Mozambique and Namibia are some of the examples. Because of their multi-faceted tasks and functions, these peacekeeping operations require a broader concept of peacekeeping, with the active participation of non-military - civilian and civilian police - components. It may involve active intervention in domestic affairs during the crucial transitional period agreed upon by the parties to the conflict.

New peacekeeping operations have raised a number of complex and controversial issues. In the current situation, for instance, can and should the use of force by peacekeepers be confined strictly to instances of self-defence or does the notion of self-defence need to be broadened to comprise not only physical self-defence of oneself and one's colleagues but also extend to the defence of the mission itself? How do we guard against its abuse? Where is the dividing line between excessive caution and the overly "robust" use of force? Peacekeepers are constantly involved in providing answers to these highly sensitive issues.

The active involvement of the United Nations in transitional national governance as well as in civil war situations provides a serious challenge to the principle of impartiality. Should peacekeepers always remain "neutral" even in the face of unspeakable violations of human rights? Should they be absolutely even-handed among the warring parties even if one of the parties represents a government recognized as a member of the United Nations? Impartiality vis-à-vis the parties becomes moot when the United Nations is asked to be the *de facto* judge or legislator in a domestic situation.

As United Nations peacekeeping operations become more complex and the military and political challenges mount, the question of command and control becomes extremely delicate. How can a multiplicity of national contingents be reconciled with the clarity of purpose and efficiency of command required? How does one cope with cultural and linguistic diversity which can be a source of numerous misunderstandings and confusion?

Burden-sharing between the United Nations and regional organizations has also become a topical subject in many United Nations peacekeeping operations. UNPROFOR in the Former Yugoslavia, for example, works closely with such bodies as the North Atlantic Treaty Organization, the Conference on Security and Cooperation in Europe and the European Union, not to mention other entities such as the United Nations High Commissioner for Refugees and the International Committee of the Red Cross. The relations with NATO have given UNPROFOR a new dimension of technical and military capability and, at the same time, has exposed the difference in their philosophy with regard to the employment of force. Reconciling such differences between the organizations concerned is of vital importance.

Moreover, keeping peace, in the form of arranging cease fires, interposing oneself between warring parties and helping to stabilize the situation on the ground has to be synchronized with efforts for diplomacy and peacemaking. Peacekeeping often means bringing about conditions for concluding a subsequent peace agreement (like in Bosnia-Herzegovina), or it can be a result of peacemaking and mediation efforts and thus be introduced only at the stage of implementing an agreement already reached (as in Cambodia). We must also be able to ensure that peacekeeping does not degenerate into the freezing of the status quo, although maintaining a precarious status quo is no mean achievement by itself (Cyprus and Croatia).

These are some of the hard questions the international community cannot avoid answering if United Nations peacekeeping is to become an even more potent instrument for international peace and a dynamic tool for security for all. While the achievements of United Nations peacekeeping are substantial, there is a long and hazardous process of trial and error before us. It is vital that we refrain from hasty judgements or utopian day-dreaming on peacekeeping operations. The international community should be steadfast in supporting peacekeeping and peacemaking efforts through the United Nations and its associated bodies, despite their present limitations; for the alternative for us is likely to be far more costly, not just in financial terms, but in human lives.

Yasushi Akashi

UNITED NATIONS PEACEKEEPING OLD AND NEW: AN OVERVIEW OF THE ISSUES

by Georges Abi-Saab

The title of this colloquium involves a reference and a referent. "New" dimensions can only be identified by reference to the "old" or "original" ones; nor can they be fully understood without knowing where they came from.

What do we mean by peacekeeping? I would suggest for the purposes of definition the combination of two criteria: one extrinsic, relating to the context and the environment which begot this new type of international activity; the other intrinsic, relating to the nature of the beast or its essential characteristics.

Peacekeeping started as an improvisation or an improvised response to a specific occasion: the Suez crisis. This response was later rationalized, generalised and reformulated in terms of a model of action to be followed in future occasions. The model was thus to a great extent conditioned by the particular circumstances which gave birth to it. To give just two examples of how the particular affected the general: In Suez the British and the French alleged, as a pretext for their invasion of Egypt, that they were intervening on behalf of the international community to protect and isolate a waterway essential to international commerce from a local war. They were in essence saying: "We intervene because there is no international police; we intervene as a *de facto* international police". When Lester Pearson --in close consultation with Dag Hammerskjöld -- later came with his proposal to create UNEF (The United Nations Emergency Force), the first UN peacekeeping Force, he

D. Warner (ed.), New Dimensions of Peacekeeping, 1-9.
© 1995 *Kluwer Academic Publishers. Printed in the Netherlands.*

used exactly the same argument and the same terms, but in reverse. By proposing the deployment of a real international police force in the area, he deprived them of their alleged pretext for being there without directly rebutting it.

Thus, an emergency practical solution to the immediate crisis could be found, without passing judgement on the actions of the parties and without prejudice to their legal contentions underlying these actions; a condition which made this solution acceptable to the parties (providing them, as it did, with a face-saving device) and permitted its quick adoption; and which was later on elevated into a governing principle of peacekeeping operations.

Another principle -- which endured for a time but is no longer observed -- prescribing that in peacekeeping forces there should be no contingents from the permanent members of the Security Council, also goes back to the creation. For when Hammerskjöld, in negotiating with the British and especially the French, asked them to withdraw from Suez in application of the General Assembly resolutions, they retorted that all he needed was to issue blue berets to their soldiers who were already there and who would thus become the international police force. Of course this solution could not have worked out for multiple reasons, particularly the non-acceptance of the territorial State, Egypt. But Hammerskjöld answered them on grounds of principle: that the inclusion of contingents from the permanent members of the Security Council would defeat the very purpose of peacekeeping operations as a tool of "preventive diplomacy" (taken in the original sense of the term when he coined it, and not that given to it by the current Secretary-General in his *Agenda for Peace*), namely to isolate regional and local conflicts from the Cold War context, or rather to prevent the Cold War from engulfing them.

Peacekeeping was thus a by-product -- albeit by way of reaction -- of the Cold War; an improvisation in the effort of the UN to transcend or bypass the constraints of the Cold War in search of a role in a specific crisis. It was modulated by this general context as well as that of the specific crisis; and later on systematised by Dag Hammerskjöld to become the sharpest tool of his "preventive diplomacy".

So much for context. Now, if we turn to examine the nature of the beast, what do we exactly mean by peacekeeping? The present Secretary-General, Boutros Boutros-Ghali, defines it in his *Agenda for Peace* in the following terms:

> "Peacekeeping is the deployment of a United Nations presence in the field, hitherto with the consent of all the parties concerned, normally involving United Nations military and/or police personnel and frequently civilians as well".

In fact, this definition has developed as a function of the ideal type of peacekeeping operations which still remains, after almost three decades, the first one, UNEF. What are the characteristics of these operations in general? First, peacekeeping operations (or forces) must have a mandate conferred by the Security Council or the General Assembly, which is usually to fulfil an international task. Now, in Suez that was easy because the task was interposition between two belligerents permitting one to withdraw; then deployment around a line and monitoring the fact that this line was not violated one way or the other. This task is purely international, it can be fulfilled in an autonomous way and it can be fulfilled by the Force without intervening in the international affairs of either party. It is a task which could be confined to the international sphere.

Peacekeeping in this sense has two main characteristics. The first is that, though carried out by armed forces, these are consensual operations. They are based on the consent of the territorial state; and that makes them different from the collective measures or sanctions provided for in Article 42 of the Charter. They also have to have the consent of the other parties to the conflict; otherwise there will be no disengagement or possibility of peaceful deployment by the UN Force. And politically they have to have the consent of the two superpowers, because the whole idea was to keep the conflict out of the Cold War, i.e. that the superpowers would accept to take the back seat and let the UN handle the crisis;

which they would do only if each knew that the other superpower would not benefit from the situation.

The other characteristic of peacekeeping -- which follows from its consensual base -- is its legally provisional nature. It was meant to serve as an emergency measure, a "fire brigade action", just to stop the fighting and to prevent it from recurring; in fact buying time for the settlement of the underlying dispute by other means. Moreover, in order to be acceptable to all parties, and provide a rapid response to the emergency, it had to be undertaken on a "without prejudice" basis, i.e. not taking a position on the parties' claims, legal positions, or on their contentions as to why they have acted the way they acted. That was left between brackets for another type of activity which came to be known as *peacemaking*, in fact the peaceful settlement of the dispute underlying the conflict, from which peacekeeping, coming first, had to be radically separated in order to preserve its consensual and provisional character.

This type of peacekeeping was subject to three legal principles, which logically derive from its essential characteristics. First, the autonomy of the Force; the Force is not meant to help one party against the other, but to fulfil an international mandate; and is accountable only to the organ which created it. But the other side of the coin is that the Force, if it has to preserve its autonomy, should also respect the autonomy of the territorial state as well as the other parties and should not intervene in their internal affairs. Finally, as the whole activity is based on consent, there should be no use of force except in self-defence.

This model, which reflects the characteristics of the crisis which begot it in the first place, fared rather well, but progressively less so as we moved into other crises; different circumstances call for different responses and varying doses of enabling mandate and governing principles. This was graphically illustrated by the case that almost broke the back of the UN, i.e. the Congo crisis of 1960 and the Congo Operation which went on for four years and which revealed two problems with the model I have just described. First, it is all well and good when the mandate can be defined in exclusively international terms, but it is very difficult in many instances to separate the internal aspects of a crisis from its international dimensions. Once the Force is deployed in a country like the Congo (now Zaire), which subsequently undergoes a breakdown of government and a constitutional crisis, there is a vacancy (or fragmentation) of power and whatever the Force does, it will somehow affect the internal balance of power; in other words, it is almost impossible not to intervene in the internal affairs even if utmost care is taken.

The other problematic question which was raised by the Congo crisis is what to do with a reluctant party which puts forth obstacles to the fulfilment by the Force of its mandate, even if it had at the beginning consented to it. This poses a dilemma to the UN: either to extend the mandate in order to achieve its purpose, at the price of transforming its nature and abandoning one or more of the principles, that which was done twice in the Congo, first when the Security Council gave the Force the right to take the initiative of using force to evacuate mercenaries and prevent civil war, and later on, through interpretation, to dismantle roadblocks; or to keep the mandate unchanged and respect the principles, and end up not fulfilling it, or not completely, as in the case of UNIFIL in Southern Lebanon.

Another shortcoming of peacekeeping operations revealed itself as time went by. Emergency measures are good antidotes for emergencies, but they also have long-term effects. The purpose of peacekeeping as I said was to contain an explosion and prevent its recurrence. In fact it was to buy time in order to settle the underlying dispute. However, as we all know, once a crisis moves from the front page of the New York Times to the inside then out, attention to it wanes as well as the pressure to do something about it. In this way, peacekeeping which started as a kind of analgesic to stop the pain, not to cure the illness, instead of buying time for peacemaking, ended up as a substitute for it, a soft option or alternative for political inaction. In the long run this proved very dangerous because putting a cover on an ongoing dispute does not make it disappear, only turn inward, becoming more inextricable and gangrenous and making for greater explosions later on, as was proved time and time again in Cyprus, the Middle East, and elsewhere.

There is another reason why this initial form of peacekeeping started to wane. As I mentioned, its prime purpose was to serve as a tool of preventive diplomacy in the Hammerskjöldian sense, not in the *Agenda for Peace* sense, i.e. to prevent the extension of the Cold War to local and regional conflicts in what we now call the Third World. However, as time went by, most of these conflicts did fall under the sway of the Cold War through the alliances that local parties had made with one or the other superpower. Thus by the mid-1960s, no conflict could be isolated from the Cold War. This was clear in the Rann Kutch conflict, the 1967 Middle East conflict, etc.

The superpowers had an interest in stopping these conflicts because they wanted to avoid confrontation. But they were not really eager to solve them because that would have necessarily meant the acceptance of the defeat of one or the other of their local allies. All they wanted and could agree on was simply to stop the fighting; and peacekeeping, as in the second UNEF in 1973, meant only freezing the conflict, an exercise in what came to be called *conflict management*, implying the acceptance of the perennial nature of these conflicts as a fatality. They were interested simply in a standstill rather than in really solving the problem; not to mention that solving the underlying problem would have reduced the dependence of the local parties on the superpowers.

This was the situation until the momentous changes of the 1980s which brought with them a new type or generation of peacekeeping operations. This new type -- which is the subject of the present colloquium -- is significantly different from its predecessor both in context and in content. As far as context is concerned, unlike initial peacekeeping which was as we have seen a by-product of the Cold War, this is a post-Cold War type of activity.

The radical change in context is reflected also in content. Thus, in the first place, while the modalities are largely the same -- still involving the deployment of troops not to fight but to stabilize a situation -- the new peacekeeping is very different in its instrumentalisation as part of a larger strategy. It reverses the complacent tendency of crisis management. Not only does it not come before peacemaking and in radical separation from it, but it is ideally part and parcel of a peacemaking package where there is an agreement, or at least an agreed framework for the settlement of the dispute along certain lines, and the peacekeeping forces are provided for as a component of this package in order to implement the agreed solution or to see to it that it is properly implemented.

Secondly -- and that is very different from the old type, though there were exceptions -- most of the crises where it has been used have been internal. The assumption that the ideal type of peacekeeping involves a purely international mandate which can be implemented in total isolation from the internal situation of the parties is completely reversed; most operations we now have are entrusted with largely internal functions, such as disarming and neutralising troops of different internal factions and consigning them to camps under UN control, repatriation and resettlement of refugees, organizing and supervising elections or referenda, and sometimes even direct administration of parts of the territory. This is a very different conception from that of original peacekeeping.

Thirdly, the nature of the activities and functions have also changed. The military dimension of the new operations, however important it may be, is not as dominant as it used to be in the old type. For example, the humanitarian dimensions can be as important, if not more in certain cases. And the span of the functions has radically widened. Not only does peacekeeping extend upstream to mesh with *peacemaking*, partaking in the implementation of an agreed framework for resolving the dispute underlying the conflict, but it also extends downstream to *peace-building*; helping create the conditions of sustainable peace after the termination of the operation. For example, UNTAG helped with drafting the new constitution in Namibia, as well as creating viable economic conditions for the resettlement of refugees, which was also done in several other cases.

These are the new tendencies and dimensions of peacekeeping. In his first annual report on the work of the Organization for the year 1991-1992, Secretary-General Boutros Boutros-Ghali, referring to Cambodia, Somalia, El Salvador and the former Yugoslavia, remarks that "new forms of conflict" call for a "global" or "integrated" approach and give rise to new forms of peacekeeping operations. Rather than new forms of conflict (they are not really), what is new is the involvement of the UN in this essentially internal type of conflict and the extent of this involvement, which call for the adaptation of the operations in their methods and configurations.

The increasing complexity of the tasks together with the great multiplication of the operations since the late 1980s have inexorably led to the complication of pre-existing problems while adding to them. Let me in conclusion mention three which are likely to figure prominently in our deliberations.

First, the resources. This is the most difficult and persistent practical problem. Since peacekeeping came as a specific response to particular crises and every operation was tailored to the situation which called for it, the search for resources came after the political decision to undertake the operation. The Secretary-General would then shop around and negotiate to get the required resources in terms of contingents, qualified personnel, logistics, disposable financial resources, etc. This was feasible when there was one operation at a time. But when there are 12 or 15 at the same time, and when some of them are about as big as all the operations of the first type put together, it is very difficult, if not impossible, to negotiate their setting up in this *ad hoc* and *a posteriori* manner. The *Agenda for Peace* speaks of standing forces, of earmarked contingents within national armies, etc.; but very little about financial resources. In fact there are worrying signs of irresponsibility on the part of the great powers in shoving the crises on to the UN and then not doing what it takes for it to handle them effectively.

The second -- and to me the most crucial -- problem, though addressed diffidently up to now, is the multiplicity of interventions in the same crisis. We are witnessing more and more situations where, in addition to the UN contingents, other forces are present in the same theatre, whether belonging to regional organizations (as in the Former Yugoslavia) or to individual countries (Somalia, Rwanda), which are not part of the UN operation nor under its command, though with its authorization. With such multiple forces under varied mandates, it is nearly impossible to deal in a rational and effective way with highly dynamic and explosive situations. Here again the problem is that the great powers, especially the United States, want the UN to adopt very daring resolutions legitimizing their intervention in certain situations, but do not trust it for the implementation of these resolutions or some of their most sensitive aspects, which they prefer to keep to themselves.

Finally, there is a rather new problem arising from the very slippery path on which some recent operations have not feared to tread, perhaps without realising it, beyond peacekeeping proper, but not exactly into sanctions under Article 42. The term *peace enforcement* is creeping in , without anybody specifying what is meant by it. To me it can only refer to situations where UN Forces are authorized to take the initiative of using force. This is a very different type of action and I do not see how it can be integrated politically or legally into peacekeeping.

I am not saying that this should not be done in any circumstance; rather that if this is done, it is no longer peacekeeping. There is a radical transformation in the nature of the operation and the requirements of success. If it has to be undertaken at all, it should be done consciously, according to plan, rather than inadvertently. But we venture here into uncharted land fraught with danger and calling for much more serious consideration.

Case Studies: Evaluations and Lessons to be Learned

UNPROFOR IN THE FORMER YUGOSLAVIA: THE MISUSE OF PEACEKEEPING AND ASSOCIATED CONFLICT MANAGEMENT TECHNIQUES

by Victor-Yves Ghebali

Since the end of the Cold War, the United Nations Organization has been engaged in a growing number of peacekeeping operations of a so-called "second generation type". Going beyond the simple interposition of a neutral third party between warring nation-states, these operations aim at materializing the principle of self determination of peoples (Namibia, Western Sahara), securing implementation of national reconciliation arrangements between an established government and guerrilla movements (Angola, Cambodia, El Salvador, Mozambique, ...), and also of protecting -- including by means of military force -- humanitarian assistance provided to civilian populations caught in the turmoil of merciless civil wars (Somalia, Yugoslavia).[1] UN intervention in intrastate conflicts is becoming more the rule than the exception in a context where peacekeeping is routinely associated with human rights, democratic institution-building and humanitarian purposes. Until now global positive achievements have been recorded in Namibia (UNTAG, 1989-90), Angola (UNAVEM I, 1990-91), Central America (ONUCA, 1989-92) and Cambodia (UNTAC, 1991-93), and more or less fair

[1] On this topic see my article "Le developpement des opérations de maintien de la paix de l'ONU depuis la fin de la guerre froide", *Le Trimestre du monde*, No.20, IVeme trimestre 1992, pp.67-85, as well as Abi-Saab, Georges. "La deuxième génération des opérations de maintien de la paix", *Le Trimestre du Monde*, Paris, 1992, vol.IV, no.20; pp.87-97.

D. Warner (ed.), New Dimensions of Peacekeeping, 13-40.
© 1995 *Kluwer Academic Publishers. Printed in the Netherlands.*

results could possibly materialize in El Salvador (ONUSAL) and Mozambique (UNOMOZ). Against this backdrop, the UN encountered four flops of major magnitude: Angola (UNAVEM II), Western Sahara (MINURSO), Somalia (UNOSOM II) and, last but not least, Yugoslavia (UNPROFOR).

The assessment of the role performed by the UN in the geopolitical territory of the former Yugoslavia has to start from three fundamental premises. First, the UN is not handling the Yugoslav conflict alone, in splendid isolation, but in conjunction with a number of regional (European, transatlantic and pan-European) intergovernmental institutions: the European Community (now the European Union); the Western European Union (WEU); the North Atlantic Treaty Organization (NATO) and the Conference on Security and Cooperation in Europe (CSCE). Second, what the UN is actually performing, within an unprecedented cooperative institutional venture, is a multifaceted action integrating peacekeeping, peace enforcement, peacemaking and preventive diplomacy -- most of those conceptual categories and conflict management techniques reviewed in Secretary-General Boutros-Ghali's *Agenda for Peace*.[2] Third, the net result of the multilateral management of the Yugoslav conflict could, so far, be summed up by a Shakespearean formula: much ado about nothing (or almost nothing) -- for it has proved to be an exercise in futility and fecklessness, based on a perverse use of peacekeeping and related conflict management techniques.

The present paper contains two parts: an analysis of the formal objectives assigned to the various techniques used for the management of the Yugoslav conflict and a critical assessment of their actual results.

[2] *Agenda for Peace*: UN Document A/47/277 - S/24111 from June 17, 1992.

The Formal Instruments and Techniques of the Multilateral Management of the Yugoslav Conflict

During the Cold War, three major parameters characterized the realm of regional international organizations in Europe (and consequently affected the political role of the UN within the European continent): bipolarity, straitjacket mandates and mutual ignorance.

Intergovernmental institutions were established within each of the competing ideological blocs and were attributed largely symmetrical functions (NATO/Warsaw Pact; European Community/Comecon); as a pan-European body, the CSCE represented the only exception to the rule during the last 15 years of the Cold War, apart form the United Nations Economic Commission for Europe (UN/ECE). Eastern- and Western-oriented institutions operated on the basis of clear-cut and straitjacket mandates: allocation of defence to NATO and the Warsaw Pact, economic integration or cooperation to the European Community and Comecon, arms control to the West European Union and human rights to the Council of Europe; given its multifaceted mandate, the CSCE provided once again the only deviant example. As a rule, all institutions performed in sheer mutual ignorance without establishing even pragmatic working relations;[3] only the CSCE followed the practice of requesting written and oral "contributions" from institutions such as UNESCO and UN/ECE. As for the United Nations, apart from the particular case of the Cyprus conflict, it systematically avoided any involvement in European affairs -- a trend respected even more after the establishment of a specific East-West channel: the CSCE.

The collapse of communism reversed the three above-mentioned parameters. The demise of the Eastern bloc's intergovernmental

[3] The rationale of East-West schizophrenia stemmed from Western reluctance to legitimize undemocratic institutions under Soviet subordination. In the case of Western organizations, the reason pertained to the variety of memberships as well as the piecemeal conceptual approach to European security.

institutions and the emergence of a new pan-European body -- the European Bank for Reconstruction and Development (BERD) -- marked the end of bipolarity. All remaining organizations undertook significant reforms which resulted in a growing overlapping of roles and functions. The CSCE was institutionalized in order to perform *inter alia* functions of cooperative security more adapted to the needs of a "whole and free Europe" stretching from "Vancouver to Vladivostok." NATO revamped its strategic doctrine, engaged in out-of-area operations on behalf of the UN, and established structured relations with its former Warsaw Pact enemies through the instrumentality of a North Atlantic Cooperation Council (NACC) and a functional cooperation program ("Partnership for Peace"). By means of the 1992 Maastricht Treaty, the European Community decided to achieve its evolution towards a "European Union" endowed with enlarged attributes, including a Common Foreign and Security Policy (CFSP) drawing on the future military capacities of the WEU. Hitherto "NATO's silent annex", the WEU admitted (as full members or observers) the other states of NATO and/or the European Union while being provided with embryonic operational capacities with a view to becoming both the military component of the European Union and NATO's European pillar. Out of a growing pan-European vocation, the Council of Europe granted membership to several countries of the former Eastern bloc, opened its activities to virtually all remaining incumbents and indulged in institutional and programmatic reforms on the basis of its Vienna Summit Declaration of 9 October 1993. Last but not least, the United Nations itself has been liberated from its European taboo and called upon to deploy a large-scale peacekeeping operation in the former Yugoslavia: UNPROFOR.

All above-mentioned institutions have formally recognized each other and established working relations (mutual representation at meetings, exchange of documents, etc.) and, sometimes, functional coordination. This new pattern was inaugurated by the CSCE's Charter of Paris for a New Europe (November 21, 1990) and confirmed the following year by

NATO's concept of "interlocking institutions",[4] before culminating in the CSCE's Helsinki Document of July 1992. The latter established what might be called an institutional armistice in so far as it stated that the CSCE could undertake peacekeeping operations either alone or by commissioning other relevant international institutions.[5] It also proclaimed that the CSCE is a regional agreement in the sense of Chapter VIII of the UN Charter.[6] In 1993 the CSCE concluded with the UN a general "Framework for Cooperation and Coordination" as well as a specific agreement for coordination of their respective field missions in Macedonia.[7]

The Yugoslav conflict soon served as privileged ground for unprecedented inter-institutional cooperation, for at least two main reasons. First, multilateral diplomacy represented, for the major powers concerned by the Yugoslav conflict, a cheap compromise -- at the lowest common denominator -- between unilateralism and non-intervention: it had the merit of preventing political (and possible military) competition in the Balkans, while providing a soothing alibi for inaction *vis-à-vis* national public opinions appalled by growing atrocities reported throughout the former Yugoslavia. Second, given that the end of bipolarity erased the longstanding obstacles which had precluded the actual implementation of Chapter VIII of the UN Charter, it would not have been wise for the UN to handle alone a conflict of such complexity in the region of the world most endowed with security institutions and crisis management resources. In any case, a pragmatic division of labor

4 See paragraph 3 of the Copenhagen Statement of June 6, 1991, paragraph 3 of the Rome Summit Declaration of November 8, 1991 and paragraph 8 of the Brussels Communiqué of December 12, 1991.

5 See paragraph 52 of Chapter III of the "Decisions" part of the CSCE Helsinki Document 1992.

6 See paragraph 25 of the "Summit Declaration" part of the CSCE Helsinki Document 1992.

7 See CSCE Communications no.108 of April 15, 1993 (Macedonia) and no.166 of June 1993 (general framework). The general framework has also been issued as UN Document A/48/185 of June 1, 1993.

has taken place between the UN and one or more of the relevant regional European organizations in the fields of peacekeeping, peace enforcement, peacemaking and preventive diplomacy.

1. Peacekeeping

The function of peacekeeping is the preserve of a United Nations peacekeeping force (UNPROFOR) drawing on NATO's logistic and, at times, military backing.

Established by Security Council resolution 743 of February 21, 1992, as an interim arrangement (12 months) pending a global political settlement, UNPROFOR's mandate initially related to Croatia. It aimed at the demilitarization of three "United Nations Protected Areas" (UNPAs) populated by Serbian majorities or sizable Serbian minorities, the monitoring of local police activities for human rights purposes and the return of displaced peoples in the UNPAs. That mandate was enlarged to include additional areas (under the control of heavily armed Serb militias) labelled "pink zones"[8], to attribute immigration and customs functions to UNPROFOR at the UNPAs' borders at international frontiers[9] and to ensure the demilitarization of the Prevlaka peninsula following the withdrawal of the Yugoslav National Army as well as the control of the strategic Peruka dam located in one of the "pink zones."[10]

When war spread to Bosnia-Herzegovina, the Security Council ruled out the deployment of a distinct peacekeeping operation adapted to the specific needs of the situation. Instead, as a makeshift solution, UNPROFOR was enlarged and its mandate extended to Bosnia-Herzegovina in order to perform, over time, three main *palliative* tasks: the protection of shipments of humanitarian assistance coordinated by the

[8] Resolution 762 of June 30, 1992.

[9] Resolution 769 of August 7, 1992.

[10] Resolution 779 of October 6, 1992.

UNHCR (which fundamentally required ensuring the security of the Sarajevo airport)[11]; the monitoring of the ban on military flights in the airspace of Bosnia-Herzegovina (a no-fly-zone)[12]; and ensuring the protection of six towns (Srebrenica, Sarajevo, Tuzla, Zepa, Gorazde, Bihac and surroundings) designated as "safe areas" for the purpose of implementing the Vance-Owen Plan and with a view to halting ethnic cleansing in those areas.[13]

The outstanding feature of UNPROFOR's operations in Bosnia-Herzegovina is certainly NATO's contribution. Following the collapse of Communism, and in the course of reflecting on its own future in the post-Cold War world, NATO considered that peacekeeping in Europe could provide one of its new *raisons d'être*. After endless French-American squabbles, NATO member states agreed to support on a case-by-case basis, including by making available Alliance resources and expertise, out-of-area peacekeeping activities under the responsibility of the CSCE (June 1992) and, likewise, to contribute to peacekeeping operations under the political and legal authority of the UN Security Council (December 1992). NATO and the UN soon formalized their relationship by means of a direct reciprocal liaison.[14] Accordingly, UNPROFOR made use of Allied personnel from NATO's Northern Army Group (NORTHAG) for its operational headquarters in Bosnia-Herzegovina and relied on NATO's radar planes (AWACS) for the daily

[11] Resolutions 758 of June 8, 1992; 761 of June 29, 1992; 764 of July 13, 1992; 770 of August 13, and 776 of September 14, 1992.

[12] Resolutions 781 of October 9, 1992; 786 of November 10, 1992; and 816 of March 31, 1993.

[13] Resolutions 819 of April 16, 1993; 824 of May 6, 1993 and 838 of June 10, 1993.

[14] See the VOS Report on "Co-operation in Peacekeeping and Peace Enforcement", North Atlantic Assembly Document AK 230 - DSC/DC (93) 6, October 1993. See also Kofi A. Annan: "UN Peacekeeping Operations and Cooperation with NATO", *NATO Review*, vol.41, no.5, October 1993, pp.3-7, and Dick A. Leurdijk: *The United Nations and NATO in Former Yugoslavia*, The Hague, Dutch Atlantic Commission, 1994, 106 p.

monitoring of the no-fly-zone. More significantly, it called upon NATO to ensure compliance with the no-fly-zone and protection of the safe areas: in April 1994, for the first time in its history, NATO ran an actual military operation out-of-area (air strikes) in support of UN Security Council resolutions; use of force in such a context was not considered as peace enforcement, but only as a backup measure for the fulfillment of humanitarian objectives.

2. Peace Enforcement

Formally acting on the basis of Chapter VII of the UN Charter, the UN Security Council established two successive embargoes: an initial arms embargo applicable to all parties to the Yugoslav conflict[15] and, when Serbia's responsibility in the outbreak of violence became blatant, a full economic embargo aimed at the rump Federal Republic of Yugoslavia composed of Serbia and Montenegro.[16] Given indisputable evidence of growing circumvention of both embargoes (especially the economic sanctions), monitoring measures were soon implemented by NATO, the WEU, the CSCE and the European Union on a bilateral or trilateral basis. Following a clear request from the Security Council to all member States "acting nationally or *in the framework of regional organizations and arrangements*"[17] to ensure that none of their exports would be diverted to Serbia/Montenegro by means of maritime shipping, NATO and the WEU jointly started, from July 16, 1993, air and sea monitoring of the Adriatic (operation "Sharp Guard"). Land monitoring of both embargoes on the Danube, a waterway through which large quantities of products, including oil, continued to enter the rump Yugoslavia, was

[15] Resolution 713 of September 25, 1991.

[16] Resolutions 757 of May 30, 1992, 787 of November 16, 1992 and 820 of April 17, 1993 (extension of the embargo to the sector of services).

[17] Resolution 787 of November 16, 1992.

jointly tackled by the CSCE and the European Union, with a contribution from the WEU. Seven "Sanctions Assistance Missions" (SAMs) were established by the CSCE, between October 1992 and February 1993, in Hungary, Bulgaria, Romania, Macedonia, Croatia, Ukraine and Albania in order to help those countries to enforce UN sanctions more stringently. A CSCE/European Union Sanctions Coordinator located in Brussels was also appointed in February 1993 and charged mainly to assess the implementation and effect of both embargoes, to coordinate enforcement of sanctions between CSCE states and to liaise with the UN Security Council Sanctions Committee.[18] The Brussels Commission of the European Union provided the CSCE with a communication infrastructure (SAMCOMM) through which communications and coordination between the SAMs and their countries were facilitated, follow-up cases of presumed breaches of sanctions were filed and evaluation reports were written for the concerned institutions (CSCE, the European Union and the United Nations Sanctions Committee).[19]

3. Peacemaking

When war erupted in Yugoslavia, none of the -- still unreformed -- European security institutions (CSCE, NATO, WEU) was really able to deal with a conflict of such nature. Being primarily an economic institution, the European Community could certainly not pretend to have more credentials than the existing security institutions: beside the fact that Yugoslavia was not even a member state, the EC lacked experience and appropriate mechanisms. However, it represented for all states a true pole of stability and attraction in post-communist Europe. Moreover, most of

[18] The latest extension of the SAMs and the Sanctions Coordinator mandates is December 31, 1994 (see the *Journal* of the fifth meeting of the CSCE Permanent Committee).

[19] See Council of Europe's Parliamentary Assembly Document 6863 of June 11, 1993. SAMCOMM submitted its first situation report on October 15, 1992.

its members were seriously envisaging furthering the integration process at the political and military levels as well as the economic level. At any rate, from the early phase of the Yugoslav conflict, the European community arrogated to itself -- with superb temerity -- the task of peacekeeping.[20] Accordingly, it convened the International Conference on Yugoslavia at the Hague (September 7, 1991), under the presidency of Lord Carrington, assisted by an Arbitration Commission (the "Badinter Commission") composed of the Presidents of five Constitutional Courts of Community member states. The Conference ended in total failure on November 5, 1991. The collapse of the peacemaking process was due to the conjunction of three main factors. First, it proceeded from the erroneous assumption "that it was *republics* that were in conflict rather than *nations*".[21] Second, the Community member states were divided on basic issues (such as peace-enforcement, self-determination of peoples and territorial integrity of states). Third, Serbia rejected the basic compromise suggested by Lord Carrington, in a draft Convention providing for the transformation of Yugoslavia into an association of sovereign and independent republics, which would have recognized the existing frontiers of those republics but also granted special status to certain ethnic groups and areas.[22] The Community peacemaking exercise lost its rationale with the adoption by the Twelve, on December 17, 1991 under overwhelming German pressure, of the Community's "Guidelines on the recognition of new states in Eastern Europe and in the Soviet Union". However, it continued to sleepwalk in the first half of 1992 in Lisbon and Brussels (under Portuguese presidency) and in the second half of the same year in London (under British presidency).

[20] See Zametica, John. "The European Community and the Yugoslav Crisis", *The Diplomatic Record, 1991-1992*, ed.by Hans Binnendijk and Mary Locke, London, Westview Press, 1992; pp.53-68.

[21] *ibid.*, pp.64-65.

[22] Text of the "Treaty Provisions for the Convention": document CPE/PRES/HAG 1280, October 24, 1991.

A new, larger and more sophisticated diplomatic exercise took over on September 3, 1992: the Geneva International Conference on the Former Yugoslavia (ICFY) which is supposed to continue until a final settlement of all the problems related to the conflict is reached. The Geneva Conference is not purely European. It is a joint venture co-chaired by the United Nations Secretary-General and the country holding the European Union's presidency; it subsidiarily associates the CSCE and the Organization of the Islamic Conference.[23] Serviced by a small Secretariat, it makes use of the former Badinter Commission for advice on legal matters. Although structured into six working groups (humanitarian issues; ethnic and national communities and minorities; succession issues; economic issues; confidence and security-building and verification measures; Bosnia-Herzegovina), it has actually focused most of its energy on the question of the status of Bosnia-Herzegovina by means of two successive aborted schemes: the Vance-Owen plan (envisaging the reorganization of Bosnia-Herzegovina into ten highly decentralized provinces, attributing 25% of the territory of this former Yugoslav republic to the Moslems and 40% to the Serbs) and the Stoltenberg-Owen Plan (envisaging the transformation of Bosnia-Herzegovina into a loose confederation of three autonomous ethnic republics authorized to secede).[24]

[23] Its operational work is managed by a steering committee co-chaired by a representative of the UN Secretary-General (initially Cyrus Vance and later Thorvald Stoltenberg) and a representative of the Presidency of the European Union (Lord Owen). The other members of the steering committee are the five permanent members of the UN Security Council, the European Union troika (the outgoing, present and forthcoming presidents of the Union), the CSCE Troika, and a representative of the Organization of the Islamic Conference.

[24] Progress reports of the Conference (up to July 1994): United Nations documents S/24795, S/25015, S/25050, S/25100, S/25221, S/25248, S/25403, S/25479, S/25490, S/25708, S/25709, S/26066, S/26233, S/26260, S/26337, S/26395, S/26486, S/26922, S/1994/64, S/1994/83, S/1994/173 and S/1994/811.

4. Preventive Diplomacy

Concerns about a possible extension of violence to other parts of the former Yugoslavia (particularly in Kosovo and Macedonia) and/or in the neighborhood (a Balkan war) pushed the CSCE -- which could afford neither peacekeeping nor peacemaking activities -- to play a pioneering role in the field of preventive diplomacy.

In the autumn of 1992 the CSCE convinced the federal government of the rump Yugoslavia -- then headed by Milan Panic -- to agree on the establishment of "Long Duration Missions" (LDMs) in those regions of Serbia whose autonomy has been abruptly abolished by the Milosevic regime: Kosovo (where Albanians represent 90% of the population), Voivodina (where several ethnic minorities existed, beginning with an important Hungarian minority) and Sanjak (a territory including a sizeable Muslim population). The LDMs were mandated to promote dialogue between the appropriate authorities and the concerned populations, to collect information on human rights violations, to establish contact points for solving problems and, finally, to assist in providing relevant information (on human rights, protection of minorities, free media and democratic elections).[25] They operated according to a formal agreement concluded on October 28, 1992 with Belgrade for an initial six month period that was subsequently prolonged by three months to June 28, 1993. The new Belgrade government which took over after Panic's fall subordinated the renewal of the LDM's mandate to the reintegration of the rump Yugoslavia (whose membership had been suspended) in the CSCE.[26] The latter preferred, however, not to

[25] See Annex 1 to *Journal*, no.2 of the 15th meeting of the Committee of Senior Officials, August 14, 1992.

[26] Yugoslavia's membership in the CSCE was suspended in July 1992: see Annex to *Journal*, no.7 of the 13th meeting of the Committee of Senior Officials, July 7, 1992, and Annex to *Journal*, no.2 of the Helsinki Summit, July 10, 1992. The United Nations General Assembly took a similar decision several months later (Resolution 47/1 of September 22, 1992).

maintain the LDMs at the price of granting political legitimization to a state guilty of violations of practically all the CSCE's fundamental values, principles and commitments.[27]

While deploying its LDMs, the CSCE simultaneously worked out preventive arrangements aimed at avoiding the spill-over of the Yugoslav conflict into countries bordering the rump Yugoslavia. But in this regard, it was bypassed by the European Union which started negotiating agreements with Hungary, Bulgaria and Albania directed at extending the action of its own Monitoring Mission to their territories. Under the circumstances, the CSCE limited its effort to the unique --but crucial -- case of the FYROM (Former Yugoslav Republic of Macedonia). In September 1992, it instituted a "Spill-over Monitor Mission to Skopje" tasked with following developments along the borders of Macedonia, establishing contacts with representatives of political parties and ordinary citizens, assessing the level of the country's internal stability as well as the possibility of conflict and unrest throughout the region and, in case of incidents, assisting in establishing the facts.

In parallel, upon a formal request from the Skopje authorities (first addressed in vain to the USA, and then to NATO): the United Nations decided to undertake a similar exercise in preventive diplomacy. The Security Council authorized the Secretary-General to deploy an infantry battalion (supported by a group of 35 military observers) to Macedonia as well as a small group of civilian police taken from UNPROFOR.[28] Later, the Security Council enlarged this nucleus by adding 300 American soldiers.[29] As the purpose of such a "UNPROFOR presence" (numbering 1200 troops) was to monitor and report on developments in the border area adjacent to Albania and Serbia/Montenegro which could undermine the internal situation or territorial integrity of Macedonia, the

[27] The UN Security Council exhorted Serbia/Montenegro, in vain, to reconsider the decision not to discontinue the LDMs' mandate (Resolution 855 of August 5, 1993).

[28] Resolution 795 of November 11, 1992.

[29] Resolution 842 of June 18, 1993.

Security Council recommended coordination with the CSCE Spill-over Mission. Accordingly, the UN and the CSCE signed, on April 14, 1993, a formal agreement providing for the weekly consultations at the level of head of mission, regular exchange of situation reports and coordination of movements. The text also commits both parties not to make public comments on their respective functioning and activities and to assist each other in cases of emergency, in particular, with regard to evacuation of personnel.[30] While both missions have a similar task of monitoring borders, the CSCE has the additional (peace-building) responsibility of contributing to the internal stabilization of the country by means of good offices.

The Actual Results of the Multilateral Management of the Yugoslav Conflict

The simultaneous operation, under the global authority of the United Nations, of peacekeeping, peace-enforcement, peacemaking and preventive diplomacy techniques is certainly impressive in its scope, sophistication and originality. However, such an operation is not based on anything resembling a strategy. What the United Nations has actually been performing is a series of uncoordinated moves amounting to: (a) an exercise in irrelevance (UNPROFOR in Croatia) and escapism (UNPROFOR in Bosnia-Herzegovina); (b) an exercise in moral injustice (arms embargo) and in ineffectiveness (economic sanctions); (c) an exercise in moral unworthiness (peacemaking chiefly through the ICFY) and (d) a useful but limited exercise in preventive diplomacy (UNPROFOR branch in Macedonia).

30 See CSCE Communication no.108 of April 15, 1993.

1. Peacekeeping: Irrelevance and Escapism

It would be unfair to argue that UNPROFOR did not have, either in Croatia or in Bosnia-Herzegovina, any positive achievements on its record. In both cases, the presence of the Blue Helmets did make a difference. Under conditions of extreme ingratitude (harassment, and suspicion from all sides) and at the expense of their lives, UN soldiers managed, by and large, to prevent resumption of full-scale hostilities in Croatia as well as to reduce the magnitude of the humanitarian disaster and somehow mitigate human suffering in Bosnia-Herzegovina. The problem is not with the Blue Helmets, but with their mandate.

In Croatia the UNPROFOR could claim that it obtained the complete withdrawal of the Yugoslav National Army (JNA) and -- as mentioned above -- that it has, so far, prevented a new full-fledged Serbo-Croat war. But before its withdrawal the JNA handed over an important quantity of weaponry to the local Serbian authorities (territorial defence and police forces); moreover, JNA's units and troops shifted to Bosnia-Herzegovina, thus contributing to the extension of the Yugoslav civil war. The bare fact is that UNPROFOR's mandate in Croatia remained unfulfilled. The Blue Helmets have been unable to achieve the demilitarization of the UNPAs and the "pink zones", to exercise customs and immigration functions at UNPA's international frontiers (which means at the borders with Bosnia-Herzegovina, the rump Yugoslavia and Hungary), to monitor the activities of the local police for human rights purposes and, last but not least, to secure the repatriation of displaced persons. Failure had to be attributed primarily to the lack of cooperation from the Serbian side. This factor is, however, only the tip of the iceberg. The crux of the matter is UNPROFOR's basic concept.

It must be recalled that UNPROFOR's conception was based on the premise of the continued existence of the Socialist Federative Republic of Yugoslavia and, thus, envisaged before Croatia's international recognition and subsequent admission to the United Nations.[31] UNPROFOR was endowed with a law-and-order mandate in view of its operating within the context of the territorial integrity of the host country (Yugoslavia), like the United Nations Interim Force in Lebanon (UNIFIL). However, the deployment of UNPROFOR actually took place after Croatia became an independent sovereign state and a member of the United Nations. Tailored to the specific features of an interstate-type conflict, UNPROFOR found itself from the start obliged to cope with a qualitatively different situation that was a complex mix of internal and international conflict. In other terms, the UN "opted for an essentially internal ring-holding, operation -- in circumstances where there was virtually no chance of it being allowed to hold the ring".[32]

Political common sense would have dictated either the non-deployment of UNPROFOR or the amendment of the latter's mandate: while international law-and-order objectives remained valid (although in the context of a different nation-state), they now needed to be supplemented by objectives related to international frontier protection. Eventually, as in the context of the Cyprus conflict, the real effect of UNPROFOR in Croatia has been the freezing, and consequently the *de facto* legitimization, of the existing status quo, to the benefit of the militarily victorious side. There is no doubt that Serbian insurgents took advantage of UNPROFOR's umbrella to transform the UNPAs and "pink zones" into a separate state (with a view to its subsequent merging with Serbia) and the cease-fire zone into an international border.[33] Like the United

[31] UN Security Council resolution 721 clearly refers to "the request by the Government of Yugoslavia for the establishment of peacekeeping operation in Yugoslavia" (second paragraph of the preamble) while admitting that the deployment of such an operation requires full consent by all parties involved (paragraph 2 of operative part).

[32] James, Alan. "The UN in Croatia: an Exercise in Futility?", *The World Today*, vol.49, no.5 May 1993, p.94.

[33] Baletic, Zvonimir. "UNPROFOR in Croatia", *Politicka Misao/Croatian Political Science Review*, vol.2, no.2, 1993; pp.50-51.

Nations Force in Cyprus (UNIFCYP), UNPROFOR in Croatia has become part of the problem as well as the solution, since it is confronted with a dilemma whose alternatives are equally unsatisfactory: sanctioning an unfair status quo (the capture of 25% of Croatia's territory) with a continuing presence or providing an incentive for renewed hostilities by withdrawing. UNPROFOR is more than an exercise in "futility" (as suggested by Alan James): given the basic conceptual flaws of its mandate, it is, more accurately, an exercise in *irrelevance*.

UNPROFOR in Bosnia-Herzegovina presents quite a different picture. In Croatia, it could be said that UNPROFOR's intervention proved to be irrelevant only *post facto*: its mandate has actually been overtaken by events which the Security Council could not have foreseen. By contrast, UNPROFOR's mandate in Bosnia-Herzegovina was deliberately conceived in irrelevant terms: as a peacekeeping operation having (for the first time in UN history) an exclusively *humanitarian* mandate. In Bosnia-Herzegovina there was no peace to keep. There was a raging merciless war -- not just a civil war, but, as Margaret Thatcher put it, "a war of aggression planned and launched from outside Bosnia, although using the Serbian militias within it"[34] -- that needed to be stopped. The rationale for a purely humanitarian mandate was twofold. On the one hand (and this could be considered as UNPROFOR's hidden agenda), the objective was to create a major *obstacle to peace enforcement*: a military intervention could put at risk the lives of neutral peacekeepers equipped with only light weapons and deployed on unfavorable terrain. On the other hand, humanitarian action represented a mere *compensation for military inaction and moral, political and military resignation* for governments (*vis-à-vis* themselves as well as public opinion). In any event, to put it more bluntly, peacekeeping was used as palliative and, thus, amounted to an exercise in escapism.

Under the circumstances, the Blue Helmets were required to perform

[34] Thatcher, Margaret. "Stop the Serbs with Air Strikes and Arms for their Adversaries", *International Herald Tribune*, May 5, 1994.

the dual role of good samaritans to distressed populations and neutral bystanders to their ordeal. UNPROFOR military neutrality allowed Serbian warlords, with the covert support of the Belgrade authorities, to capture up to 70% of Bosnia-Herzegovina's territory and to achieve its ethnic cleansing at the expense of 250,000 lives, over half a million refugees and 1.3 million displaced persons. Humanitarian assistance (which prolonged their agony but did not help them to escape) was not what besieged civilians needed most. In any event, UNPROFOR's Blue Helmets unwillingly became by proxy wardens of a global slaughterhouse where warlords could shoot civilian populations (provided with humanitarian assistance) practically at leisure, except for in Sarajevo since NATO's ultimatum of February 1994. Willy nilly, by virtue of its mere passivity UNPROFOR became an accomplice to a genocide enjoying a *de facto* international legitimization.

Moreover, and what is even worse, the numerous extensions of UNPROFOR's size and mandate in Bosnia-Herzegovina were adopted by the UN Security Council only in response to unfolding events. In all cases, the Security Council's resolutions issued ambivalent and incoherent messages which the aggressors rightly decoded as a license to further pursue the same path. According to the conjuncture, UN resolutions were drafted in language aimed at: not irking the Russians too much, assuaging Western concerns about not becoming too involved, or simply responding to outraged international public opinion; moreover, although resolutions threatening air strikes against aggressors and authorizing a war crimes tribunal were directed at the Serbs, their language remained neutral and applicable to any of the warring factions.[35] The blatant discrepancy between words and deeds is best illustrated by the fact that as of June 1994, not less than 1,696 violations of the no-fly-zone were officially reported by the United Nations[36] and that NATO's actual air strikes

[35] See Coll, Steve. "Original Sin and a 4-year Tale of War", *International Herald Tribune*, April 21, 1994.

[36] See UN Document S/1994/5/Add.37, of June 7, 1994.

have just been pinprick attacks against tactically useless targets causing insignificant damage. In sum, under frequent threat, harassment, intimidation and attack from all sides (who accuse them either of partiality or of undignified neutrality) UNPROFOR's Blue Helmets are experiencing a permanent loss of face and becoming hostages of the aggressors as well as of the inability of the Security Council to go beyond a daily political strategy. Because of the Security Council permanent members' procrastination and fecklessness, UNPROFOR is, sadly, illustrating one of the most elementary rules of basic politics axiomized by Hans Morgenthau: "Never put yourself in a position from which you cannot retreat without losing face and from which you cannot advance without grave risks."[37] NATO's Secretary-General Manfred Woerner, for his part, summarized this rule in the following terms: "threaten only if you are determined to implement the threat," while "avoid[ing] situations where your own troops became hostages."[38]

2. Peace Enforcement: Moral Injustice and Ineffectiveness

The significance and effects of the arms embargo have to be carefully distinguished from those of economic sanctions.

The imposition of the arms embargo at the early stage of the Yugoslav conflict, in September, 1991 was certainly appropriate. It has helped to limit the scale of killings and to prevent all sides from introducing sophisticated weaponry in the fighting areas and in the Balkan region. Lifting that embargo now, it is often said, would be an irresponsible move: it would contribute to intensifying and prolonging violence among warring parties and also to paving the way for the internationalization of

[37] Quoted by Krauthammer, Charles. "Bosnian Venture in a Wing and a Prayer", *International Herald Tribune*, April 16-17, 1994.

[38] Speech at the Seminar on "Peacekeeping in Europe" organized by the Spanish Centre for International Relations (El Escorial, October 29, 1993).

the conflict (beginning with probable Russian support to the Serbs). These arguments are not unsound. However, they should be assessed against the background of moral considerations. The embargo should have been lifted when it became clear which side started the war and committed the largest and most outrageous violations of human rights and humanitarian law. As a matter of principle, it was questionable to adopt a purely neutral stand *vis-à-vis* "warring parties" when there were clear victims and clear aggressors. The real point was actually the unbalanced effects of the embargo: the latter could not harm the Serbian side (as the inheritor of JNA's heavy armaments) while it would inevitably cripple the less-armed (and mainly with light arms) Muslim side. Such an imbalance protected the starting advantage of the Serbs and greatly facilitated the seizure of 70% of Bosnia-Herzegovina and the implementation of ethnic cleansing. The real issue has been admirably summarized by Secretary-General Woerner in the following cursory statement: "if you cannot or do not want to help the victim of aggression, enable him to help himself".[39] Finally, the arms embargo is not only morally unjust, it is also unjustifiable from a legal point of view since it deprives a United Nations member state that is a victim of aggression of making full use of its self-defence right as provided for in article 51 of the Charter.[40]

In sharp contrast with the arms embargo, the economic sanctions against the rump Yugoslavia could be said to be plainly justified in moral terms (as a stigmatization of unlawful behavior) and political terms (as a means of diplomatic pressure on a key actor in the conflict). The only trouble is their basic ineffectiveness: "economic sanctions are not worth the paper they are written on when they are not backed by credible military sanctions".[41] In other words, economic sanctions used as an

[39] *Ibid.*

[40] Among the many explicit or implicit reasons invoked for not lifting the arms embargo is American fear that this could facilitate the abrogation of embargoes against Iraq, Libya and Haiti.

[41] Sharp, Jane M.O. "Intervention in Bosnia - the Case For", *The World Today*, vol.49, no.2, February 1993, p.31.

end in themselves (and not, like in the Gulf War against Saddam Hussein, as a first warning signal) cannot, by definition, succeed: all previous similar experiences in modern history have proven barren. Moreover, if directed against an undemocratic power, economic sanctions penalize the population but not the regime which, by playing the tune of national pride, gets new legitimacy. Finally, in order to be really effective sanctions have to be universally respected: in fact, economic embargoes are routinely circumvented for purposes having to do with simple profit, unduly high costs for third parties (especially neighboring countries or external major commercial partners),[42] or traditional historical or cultural affinities. In any case, international economic sanctions are normally used for retribution, compulsion and deterrence.[43] In the case of the rump Yugoslavia they are only fulfilling a (moral) retribution function; from the point of view of compulsion and, in all likelihood, of deterrence of future wrongful behavior, their effect is just nil.

3. Peacemaking: Moral Indignity

Among the various techniques used for the multilateral management of the Yugoslav conflict, peacemaking is no doubt the one whose misuse can be considered as the most undignified on moral grounds since it amounts to imposing on the victim the obligation to cooperate with the carving up of his own territory. The spirit of the political settlement envisaged in peacemaking proposals tabled so far (the Vance-Owen Plan, the Stoltenberg Plan, the Common Action Plan, the Contact Group's Plan...) unequivocally violates the basic principles of the United Nations Charter

[42] See UN document A/48/573 - S/26705 of November 8, 1993 and especially, the Council of Europe's Parliamentary Assembly Document 6979 of December 15, 1993.

[43] See Nossal, Kim Richard. "International Sanctions as International Punishment", *International Organization*, vol.43, no.2, Spring 1989; pp.301-322.

as well as CSCE basic values and commitments. Those proposals are outrageous in the sense that they tend: (a) to reward aggression by legitimizing frontier changes achieved by means of military conquest; (b) to carve up the territory of a sovereign independent state belonging to the United Nations against its own expressed free will (in line with the precedents such as the 1936 Laval-Hoare Plan and the 1938 Munich "settlement"), while the UN Security Council resolutions ritually reaffirm "the sovereignty, territorial integrity and political independence of the Republic of Bosnia-Herzegovina";[44] (c) to help legitimize the creation of ethnically pure nation-states in Europe. In sum, all ongoing peacemaking efforts are based on the implicit premise of an *unjust peace* at the expense of the victim -- with the awkward consequence, for the international community, of having to send troops to guarantee the results of... ethnic cleansing. Although morally hard to swallow, peace at the price of injustice might be acceptable if it provided the least bad of the worst options under the circumstances and if it were conducive to real peace. The trouble is that all peacemaking schemes are, in all likelihood, unimplementable, with neither side being really satisfied and, thus, ready to respect them. Seen in that perspective, peacemaking efforts become a means for presiding over the simple destruction of Bosnia-Herzegovina.

Such a disastrous misuse of peacemaking can be attributed to three main reasons: the erroneous working hypothesis assumption adopted by peacemakers that Croats and Serbs really accept the continued existence of a Muslim nation-state, the eagerness of peacemakers (who ruled out military use of force) to achieve a diplomatic settlement at any price; and finally the piecemeal approach to solving a conflict which requires a global solution.[45]

[44] Among the latest examples, see resolution 900 of March 4, 1994.

[45] For more on this point see Djuric, Ivan. "L'au-delà de la guerre dans l'ex-Yougoslavie", *Politique étrangère*, 1994, no.1, p. 922.

4. Preventive Diplomacy: A Limited Right Step

Missions established by the United Nations and the CSCE in FYROM are the only positive element of the multilateral management of the Yugoslav conflict. Both Missions are innovative and forward looking. The UNPROFOR "presence" in Macedonia is the first operation of preventive diplomacy in United Nations history -- an operation deployed, in fact, with the consent of only one of the potential parties to a dreaded conflict. Besides, with its Spill-over Mission in Skopje, the CSCE is demonstrating that it has a real comparative advantage over NATO or the WEU in the emerging field of preventive diplomacy. In any event, the establishment of the two Missions represented the only forward move taken by the international community in the framework of the management of the Yugoslav conflict -- the only step aimed at coping with anticipated and not already existing growing pains.

Such a step seems, however, to have a rather limited scope. First, it has not been coordinated with any peacemaking or military peace enforcement processes: the FYROM case has been tackled on its own merits, with no visible connection with a global peace package (encompassing Croatia, Bosnia-Herzegovina and Kosovo as well); moreover, in case of actual fighting, UNPROFOR simply has no mandate to intervene and its troops are supposed to leave the territory at once. Second, the functions of the UN and/or the CSCE Missions in FYROM are early warning (monitoring the situation at the borders), deterrence by virtue of their presence and good offices at an internal level (defusing inter-ethnic tensions): while early warning and good offices have been proceeding fairly well so far, it is clear that 1,200 foreign troops do not offer more than a token military presence and not real deterrence. Third, Greece's irresponsible policy *vis-à-vis* FYROM,[46] which is undermining the painstaking and fragile work of the two Missions, has so far been met

[46] A policy which culminated with the instoration of an economic embargo in April 1994.

by sluggish rather than resolute responses from the international community in general and the USA in particular: Washington, which has recognized FYROM without, however, accrediting an Embassy to it, is bowing to an effective Greek lobby. In a nutshell, the Yugoslav conflict is, unfortunately, not being managed in the same time frame in which it is occurring.[47]

Anatomy of a Global Failure

It could be argued that the multilateral management of the Yugoslav crisis was not that catastrophic. Indeed, beside the mitigation of civilian populations' suffering, the conflict has been prevented from spilling over to other areas of the former Yugoslavia or degenerating into a Balkan war, the political cohesion of the European Union has been preserved, and Washington-Moscow relations have stood firm. Such arguments are certainly valid, but have only a relative value. First, the Yugoslav conflict is a series of interconnected time bombs of which only one (Slovenia) has been defused: two are still exploding in Croatia and Bosnia-Herzegovina while two others could be activated at any moment in Kosovo and Macedonia (in the latter case possibly igniting a Balkan war). Second, the European Union avoided the renationalization of its member states' diplomacies, but at a considerable price: on the one hand, by demonstrating that a "European identity" (in foreign policy as well as security and defence matters) could only be wishful thinking, on the other hand, by trampling underfoot its declared basic values and principles through the elaboration and sponsoring of plans for the carving up of Bosnia-Herzegovina. Third, with or without contentions about the Yugoslav conflict, the course of US-Russian relations is less dependent on the Yugoslav conflict than on the evolution of the internal situation in

[47] See Jim Hoagland's column in *The International Herald Tribune* of April 31, 1994.

Russia. Above all, there remains the devastating fact that conflict management guided by procrastination, irresolution and escapism has thrown discredit on all managers and management techniques and sent the wrong signals throughout Europe and the international system at large.

Discredit has fallen down higgledy-piggledy on: international institutions, European powers and the USA as well as on the fundamental principles and ideals of minimum civilized international community. As stated by Senator Joseph Biden "...we have weakened -- and indeed disgraced -- the institutions of international security at a moment where those principles and organizations might have been strengthened in preparation for a new era of global challenge".[48] This statement is valid for both collective security and collective defense institutions: in this regard a constantly humiliated UN and a constantly mouse-roaring NATO certainly are the most serious casualties. The very technique of peacekeeping has lost most of its appeal and, as Jeanne Kirkpatrick put it, the idea of collective security might have been spoiled for another generation.[49] Equally totally deflated is the myth of a Europe pretending to be "a superpower in the making." Maastricht Europe having chosen "myopie, surdité et bavardage"[50] instead of real action, is in a sense dying in Sarajevo. Finally, the Yugoslav conflict has confirmed that the USA is stepping back from Europe and is unwilling to assume the basic responsibilities inherent to leadership.

At the root of the collective mesmerization of the Western world is the bare fact that liberal pot-bellied democracies have lost much of their taste for effort and for risk. They are unwilling to enter into a military confrontation if it has to cost anything. They have seemingly forgotten that security of civilized states is not dependent only upon direct material

[48] Statement on the Senate floor, July 30, 1993 - quoted in the Van Vlijmen Report on "The Bosnian Tragedy": North Atlantic Assembly Document AK 228 DSC (93) 9, October 1993, p.12.

[49] *International Herald Tribune* of May 9, 1994.

[50] Morin, Edgar. "Quelle guerre, quelle paix?", *Le Monde*, June 2, 1994.

and narrow interests (defense of national territory, access to strategic economic resources, etc.), but also upon interest having to do with moral standards and global order in the international system (which means democracy, prosperity and peace in the world at large). Likewise, they have been disregarding the elementary political maxim according to which security always comes at a price and "peace can only be maintained by the strong".[51] The fact is that genuine statesmen are not generated any more by liberal democracies; in the latter now emerge only politicians obsessed by daily or at best short-term interests: opinion polls and electoral consultations. Politicians might argue that they are merely following the will of the people. But in representational democracies it is not for the people as such to decide. Leadership implies *first* making decisions and *then* seeking public approval, not the other way around. Although the Yugoslav case provided a paradigmatic case in which the most basic and highly-praised Western values and principles were objectively violated, Western reaction was not at all commensurate to the magnitude of the challenge. Feckless and incoherent responses are all the more appalling in that it was for the defense of those values and principles that Western democracies straightforwardly fought communism, for more than four decades -- and defeated it.

Be that as it may, the ill-management of the Yugoslav conflict is generated in post-communist Europe the most depressing political signals possible: war can be an acceptable instrument of national policies; territorial conquests by means of brutal military aggression can be achieved with full impunity; forceful creation of ethnically homogeneous nation-states can obtain collective legitimization. Not only has Europe's political Pandora's Box been opened and nearly emptied, but, regretfully, nobody seems either able or willing to pay the price for sealing it up.

At the present stage (mid-1994), there seem to be three main broad options. The first is that of *washing hands* -- which means withdrawing

[51] According to Secretary of State George C.Marshall quoted in the Vlijmen report, *op.cit.*, p.8.

UNPROFOR's troops and letting war continue until the total military defeat of the Muslims or mutual exhaustion of the warring parties. The second option is maintaining pressure on the Muslims to compromise in order to get peace at the least bad possible terms for them : *unjust peace* is precisely the option followed heretofore.

The third one is a *limited military option* implying significant air strikes against Serbian militias. Such an option would be used not in view of rolling back the Serbs, but for the purpose of influencing the behavior of all parties at the negotiation table. When envisaging military options, it is fundamentally wrong to think in all-or-nothing terms : what is really needed is a certain amount of use of force as well as a *credible* threat of larger-scale operations in support of a politically and morally fairer global political settlement. Indeed, the real choice is not between military intervention or diplomatic negotiation. In excluding the perspective of a military option, peace-makers only succeed in *undermining* the potentialities and effectiveness of the diplomatic option -- which became, for all parties, less appealing and rewarding. Is such an option feasible at an acceptable cost? The answer could only be political. However, in purely military terms, risks do not seem to be as excessive as generally alleged : Serbian militias are using unsophisticated and even outdated weaponry; mobility of their artillery is definitely not an asset in mountainous ground and their military victoires have essentially been achieved against underarmed adversaries (and often just civilian populations). In any event, the artillery threatening Sarajevo could be destroyed in some 48 hours by means of real and resolute air strikes.[52]

Given that it bears the risk of escalation and the intervention of third parties, the military option is clearly not an ideal one. Actually, there exists no good option for the halting and settlement of the Yugoslav conflict. However, in a long-term perspective, the price of military non-intervention will certainly be more costly than that of military

[52] See the outspoken point of view of French Admiral Antoine Sanguinetti: "Les alibis militaires," *Le Monde* of June 10, 1994.)

intervention. This is because the real stakes involved in the Yugoslav conflict are not only political, but *civilizational* : the conflict has been marked by a degree of barbary unknown in Europe since the end of World War II. The Yugoslav conflict is not just a Balkan affair. It challenges the essence and meaning of the most precious values upon which the West has established its stability, prosperity, political credibility and moral authority since the end of World War II. If the West sticks to the position that United Nations and CSCE principles are applicable in the world at large but not in the territories of the former Yugoslavia, then one must fear that the worst is still to come in Europe.

THE UNITED NATIONS IN CAMBODIA AND THE NEW PEACEKEEPING

by Steven Ratner*

The United Nations' two-year presence in Cambodia marked a high point of a trend since the late 1980s towards new and expansive forms of peacekeeping. This second generation of, or "new" peacekeeping, seeks not to supervise truces between warring armies, but to assist parties in implementing peace accords that comprehensively settle an interstate or internal conflict. Although the new phenomenon has historical antecedents in certain League of Nations operations (e.g. the Saar) as well as classic UN peacekeeping and other unusual UN missions (e.g. abandoned plans for Trieste and the operations in West Iran and the Congo), it formally began with the United Nations Transition Assistance Group (UNTAG) in Namibia. Others followed shortly thereafter elsewhere, such as election missions in Nicaragua and Haiti and a multifaceted mission in El Salvador. By 1990, with negotiations hopelessly deadlocked over ending Cambodia's long war, the five permanent members of the Security Council began negotiations towards an unprecedented role for the UN in

* This paper is derived from the author's book, *The New Peacekeeping: Building Peace in Lands of Conflict After the Cold War*, New York: St. Martin's Press, 1995 (which also contains full citations). Portions appear in "The Cambodia Settlement Agreements", 87 *American Journal of International Law* 1 (1993); and "The United Nations in Cambodia: A Model for Resolution of Internal Conflicts?" in *Enforcing Restraint: Collective Intervention in Internal Conflicts*, Council on Foreign Relations Press, 1993.

D. Warner (ed.), New Dimensions of Peacekeeping, 41-67.
© 1995 *Kluwer Academic Publishers. Printed in the Netherlands.*

a member state, a plan codified in the Paris accords and realized with the United Nations Transitional Authority in Cambodia (UNTAC).

UNTAC AND THE PARIS AGREEMENTS

As originally envisioned by the Permanent Five, UNTAC's mission was to create the two key prerequisites for a free and fair election in Cambodia - a peaceful situation on the ground and a politically neutral environment. The first would be accomplished through the deployment of a massive UN military component. The second, however, necessitated a totally new role for the UN due to the factions' inability to agree on a formula for sharing power pending elections. The UN would act as an "authority" to sit above the two competing governments -- the large administrative apparatus of the State of Cambodia (SOC), which controlled 90% of Cambodian territory, and smaller organs set up by the resistance factions in areas they occupied -- and undertake any action needed to create political neutrality. The Five invented the idea of a Supreme National Council (SNC) to include representatives from all four factions and serve as the unique, legitimate authority in Cambodia -- also above the two governments -- until the formation of a government following elections. The SNC's primary purpose, as envisioned in the Agreement, was to delegate to UNTAC the authority needed to implement the settlement.

The peace agreements described in detail UNTAC's relationships to the SNC and the existing regimes and its tasks, i.e. the depth and breadth of its power. The depth of UNTAC's authority was stipulated as follows: it had to comply with the SNC's advice on any aspect of the settlement (except electoral matters, where UNTAC's power was plenary) if (a) the SNC spoke unanimously or Prince Sihanouk provided the advice on the Council's behalf; and (b) the advice was "consistent with the objectives of the present Agreement" *as determined by the chief of UNTAC*, the Secretary-General's Special Representative. If the SNC did not provide advice to UNTAC or its views were incompatible with the goals of the Agreement, the Special Representative retained the prerogative to act as he wished. This formula struck a balance between the need to respect Cambodian wishes and the urgency of implementing the settlement, but clearly gave the final word as a legal matter regarding execution of the settlement to the UN.

The breadth of UNTAC's authority included, most importantly, military operations, civil administration, organization and conduct of elections, and human rights monitoring. UNTAC's *military assignment* included verifying the withdrawal of Vietnamese troops; monitoring a cease-fire; supervising the regroupment, cantonment, and demobilization of the factional armed forces; receiving and guarding the weapons and equipment from cantoned forces; monitoring the cessation of outside assistance; interacting with neighboring governments; destroying caches of weapons; assisting with POW exchanges; and contributing to mine clearance.

In the area of *civilian administration*, the peace plan called for UNTAC to control, oversee, and work through the existing regimes according to a three-tiered scheme:

- First, all administrative organs in the areas of foreign affairs, national defense, finance, public security, and information (the five areas central to fair elections) were to be placed "under the direct control of UNTAC." The Special Representative could exercise whatever control was necessary to ensure their neutrality, including through binding directives.
- Second, UNTAC maintained "supervision or control" over any other governmental components that "could directly influence the outcome of elections," such as agencies responsible for education, agriculture, and communications -- activities that could, if administered in a partisan manner, impinge on electoral neutrality. Civilian police and judicial processes would also operate under such supervision or control in order to protect law and order as well as human rights.

- Third, the least degree of intervention was reserved for those agencies that UNTAC judged "could continue to operate in order to ensure normal day-to-day life in Cambodia." These organs, charged with less politicized matters such as cultural affairs, would not be subject to supervision or control, but UNTAC could conduct investigations to ascertain if they were subverting the settlement's objectives and take corrective steps.

Lest any doubt about the Special Representative's authority remain, the Agreement specified that, with respect to all governmental entities, he could insert UN personnel with access to all operations and documents and require the removal of any Cambodian personnel.

UNTAC's *electoral responsibilities* were even broader. Because of the mistrust among the factions, UNTAC was given direct responsibility for organizing and conducting elections. Moreover, under the accords, UNTAC was not beholden to the SNC -- even if it spoke unanimously -- with respect to elections. UNTAC was to establish laws and procedures, set a timetable, register voters and parties, organize and conduct the polling, arrange for foreign observation, and certify the elections. Its mandate thus surpassed that of the three most recent instances of electoral oversight: Namibia, Nicaragua and Haiti.

UNTAC was also given a central part in implementing the *human rights* provisions of the Paris accords, which were critical to the settlement in view of the atrocities of the Khmer Rouge and the SOC's violation of human rights. UNTAC was charged with monitoring human rights conditions, responding to violations, and conducting a large-scale education program. The goals were to prevent a climate of fear from tarnishing the election and to foster a long-term consciousness about human rights.

The Special Representative also had overall authority under the Paris accords for the repatriation of approximately 370,000 Cambodians who had fled the country during its years of war, the vast majority of whom were living in camps in Thailand. The accords gave UNHCR operational control due to its longstanding experience. The UN's last major task was to assist with the most immediate tasks of the economic rehabilitation of Cambodia after over two decades of war. It would assess the country's needs and coordinate the receipt of foreign assistance.

UNTAC'S HANDICAP: IDENTIFYING THE EXOGENOUS CONSTRAINTS

In order to understand and evaluate UNTAC's performance as a second-generation peacekeeping operation, a prerequisite intellectual task must be undertaken: to isolate the exogenous constraints upon the functioning of UNTAC that were unique to Cambodia.

1. Fragile Peace, Fragile Consent

Though it was the culmination of years of intensive negotiations, the signature of the Paris accords did not coincide with a desire by the Cambodian factions, in particular the SOC and Khmer Rouge, for peace. Indeed, they ultimately accepted the Five's plan primarily because of external pressure upon them. This opposition to peace undermined the consent critical to peacekeeping and meant that key participants had competing conceptions of how the accords would affect them.

This often illusory consent manifested itself principally in the active resistance of the Khmer Rouge and the SOC to UNTAC whenever it sought to execute its mandate contrary to their fundamental interests. The Khmer Rouge feared the loss of control over territory and people that would result from UN entry into its zones and demobilization of its forces. For that reason, in June 1992, it refused to regroup, canton, disarm, and partially demobilize its army. The SOC, too, opposed UNTAC control, and seized upon the Khmer Rouge's refusal to disarm as a justification for resisting UNTAC. By late 1992 and early 1993, the resistance of the two key belligerents had turned lethal, as the Khmer

Rouge massacred scores of ethnic Vietnamese and the SOC began killing some opposition party officials. In addition, this poor quality of consent left UNTAC to undertake its duties in a war scenario, precisely opposite to that preferred for peacekeeping operations.

Moreover, the actors in the process had inconsistent perspectives towards the core of the settlement: the relationship among the SNC, UNTAC, and the SOC. The SOC emphasized its own authority recognized under the Paris accords, noting that it still controlled the governmental apparatus, even if the SNC embodied Cambodian sovereignty. The Khmer Rouge saw the SNC as the only national entity with their participation and thus the only legitimate source of power, with UNTAC as its agent and the SOC powerless. And UNTAC saw the SNC as an important reconciliation body where it hoped many decisions could be made. Aggravating this situation was the erratic attitude of Prince Sihanouk, who failed to cooperate with UNTAC or assert leadership within the SNC as hoped.

2. A Shattered Country

Cambodia's physical infrastructure -- such as roads, electrical capacity, and telecommunications -- operated at levels found in the rest of Southeast Asia decades earlier. Into this shattered land the signatories to the Paris accords asked the UN to insert tens of thousands of troops and civilians. As a result, the UN needed to devote significant resources and time to the most basic administrative backbone of UNTAC, such as housing, water, and telephones. Cambodia's human devastation also taxed UNTAC. It had trouble locating qualified local staff for its own needs. And when it sought to execute control over the SOC, it found untrained Cambodian bureaucrats in need of extensive education to carry out UNTAC's directives.

3. Limited Interests, Competing Crises

After the signature of the Paris accords, most states viewed Cambodia as "the UN's problem," which essentially meant the Secretary-General's problem. Cambodia did not receive the sustained attention of the international community, which was focusing on more pressing crises in Somalia and the former Yugoslavia. While the Security Council's votes suggested an ironclad international consensus in favor of the Paris accords, the Council's members did not match it with a high-level commitment that might have put additional weight behind UNTAC's actions. Furthermore, the troop donor states constrained UNTAC, as their attitude affected the limits to which UNTAC could push the idea of self-defense -- always allowed under consensual peacekeeping.

Beyond the member states, the UN's Department of Peacekeeping Operations (DPKO) confronted numerous other crises during UNTAC's time in Cambodia. The immediate and far worse humanitarian disasters in Bosnia and Somalia required sustained attention. DPKO also had responsibility for elections in Angola and the ensuing fighting, a new operation in Mozambique, ONUSAL's complex work, and the older first-generation missions in Cyprus, the Golan Heights and elsewhere.

The international community thus decided to deploy UNTAC despite -- as well as because of -- the Cambodians' refusal to lay aside their differences and cooperate fully with it. The Council kept UNTAC there notwithstanding serious opposition to its work by the two armed elites in Cambodia. Member states could see no other realistic option, convinced as they were that withdrawal would mean disaster for Cambodia and the UN.

UNTAC IN ACTION

1. Deployment

In order to deploy the mission, both UN Headquarters and UNTAC had to recruit large numbers of civilian and military personnel and procure and transport enormous quantities of materiel. But despite outstanding UN staff work, logistical shortcomings hindered the operation throughout its tenure. While the military force, sent by member states, and the repatriation unit, relying on its personnel already on site, deployed rapidly, other components deployed more slowly, including the civilian police (CIVPOL) and the civil administration and human rights components. This delay stemmed from the late choice of Yasushi Akashi as the Special Representative and the lack of a complete plan for staffing the most unusual part of UNTAC, the civil administration component. Electoral preparation began before UNTAC's arrival, with a group of officials, building on the UN's long experience in elections, drafting the election law and planning the logistics.

The delay in deployment, especially of the civil administration component, proved costly. During the early months, in what has been called UNTAC's "honeymoon period," the SOC seemed more amenable to UNTAC civil administrative control. Yet UNTAC lacked the resources to implement this part of its mandate. UNTAC's inability to exercise control fuelled Khmer Rouge suspicions that UNTAC would not neutralize the SOC. This gave the Khmer Rouge a convenient excuse for withdrawing from the peace process, one that even their opponents abroad found somewhat justifiable. But once the Khmer Rouge had withdrawn, the SOC saw UNTAC's efforts at control as one-sided. When UNTAC finally had the staff for better supervision, the SOC had turned especially recalcitrant.

2. Executing the Settlement Despite Eroding Consent

a) The Quest for a Peaceful Country. UNTAC's mandate in this area was frustrated primarily by the refusal of the Khmer Rouge to canton, disarm, and demobilize its forces. The guerrillas asserted that the Paris accords were not being implemented properly insofar, they stated, as Vietnamese troops remained in Cambodia and the SOC had not surrendered power to the SNC. Diplomatic efforts to return the Khmer Rouge to the fold were ultimately unsuccessful. While some argued that UNTAC should have forced its way into the Khmer Rouge zones, political support for such a course never materialized. As a result of this non-compliance, the bulk of UNTAC's military component became more of a presence than any type of supervisor.

By the end of 1992, UNTAC had abandoned hope of supervising any demobilization and focused instead on the military's role in supporting the elections by deploying military units near population centers, UN electoral officials, and candidates. As violence by the Khmer Rouge and the SOC increased, the component provided armed escorts to electoral workers. During the elections, the military guarded polling sites. The units not part of the large battalions continued to remain busy with activities such as observation, mine clearance, and road and bridge repair.

CIVPOL, whose mandate was to supervise the police of the factions, had very mixed results. It investigated many crimes, although with inconsistent success in identifying culprits. It was also plagued by serious internal problems. Many donor states lacked any tradition of police respect for citizens or accused criminals, and did not send their best officers in any case. Many complaints by Cambodian citizens against UNTAC stemmed from inappropriate behavior by CIVPOL members that tarnished UNTAC's image with the populace. Other components also routinely criticized CIVPOL for incompetence.

b) Creating a Neutral Political Environment. The civil administration component had the most unprecedented challenge in UNTAC -- to exercise control, supervision, and oversight over the factional governments in the zones they controlled. For most of Cambodia, this meant asserting authority over the incumbent State of Cambodia. UNTAC established seven branches in Phnom Penh and sent representatives to Cambodia's provinces. Five of the branches oversaw the areas intended for "direct control" - foreign affairs, defense, information, security, and finance; a "specialized control" branch followed other parts of the SOC's apparatus that could affect electoral neutrality; and an investigations section was formed as well. The control to be exercised depended directly upon the limited size of the component, as UNTAC officials quickly concluded that full "direct control" would have required dozens of UN officials in the SOC's ministries. UNTAC thus decided to concentrate on those aspects of the civil administration with the greatest impact upon the elections.

Despite these policies, the nature of the State of Cambodia apparatus stymied UNTAC's work on all fronts. As a typical communist government, party and state were united; key government officials also served as party functionaries. When UNTAC tried to oversee a state agency, decisions would simply move to party channels. Beyond this, like many Asian bureaucracies, neither the SOC nor the party undertook decisions through formal processes such as meetings accompanied by pre- and post-decisional memoranda. Moreover, the SOC was an inherently corrupt institution; many civil servants had no loyalty to anything but money, family or party.

The component made a start on UNTAC's duties under the Paris accords, but suffered due to the SOC's intransigence. It eliminated some blatant acts of corruption and dissuaded others through monitoring, improved the functioning of some ministries through oversight and technical assistance, and helped start a process of creating a working governmental bureaucracy. It drafted various codes affecting civil servants, but used its other powers under the Paris accords judiciously.

UNTAC removed a handful of corrupt officials, but through a quiet request to the SOC leadership, avoiding any public firings. Similarly, its directives for corrective action took the form of requests, not orders. The SOC often ignored them, asserting lack of conclusive evidence.

By early 1993, UNTAC abandoned hope of neutralizing the SOC bureaucracy, focusing on the most egregious cases and challenging the SOC much more directly by deploying "Control Teams" that would arrive unannounced at a provincial government office and search it. As a result, UNTAC uncovered proof of SOC culpability for attacks on opposition leaders and intimidation of the population. Nonetheless, before the elections took place, Akashi admitted that the neutral political environment had not materialized.

c) The Electoral Mandate. The electoral component's imposing mandate -- to organize and conduct the elections -- necessitated detailed planning and execution. The component assumed a rather low-key role during the first nine months of UNTAC's operation, laying the groundwork for the elections. Although the Khmer Rouge would not allow it into its areas, the SOC did not impede UNTAC's efforts to set up the elections (which the SOC assumed it would win). The registration of voters, which took place from October 1992 to February 1993, was a true success; over 4,6 million people, nearly all those eligible, registered.

By early 1993, as the failure of the military and civilian control mandates sunk in, UNTAC focused nearly all its energies on the elections. It ultimately recruited 50,000 Cambodians and 1000 foreigners to man the approximately 1600 polling stations. It undertook a nationwide campaign through radio, television, and other media to convince the population of the secrecy of their vote; this effort responded to voter intimidation, primarily by the SOC. Indeed, this media campaign became the linchpin of a fair election in the absence of a neutral political environment.

Despite increased violence in the two months before the elections, UNTAC proceeded with the polling, which took place on May 23-28,

1993. To the great surprise of many, no significant violence marred the elections. Nearly 90% of registered voters turned out at fixed and mobile stations, voting peacefully and with full preservation of ballot secrecy. The royalist opposition, FUNCINPEC, received 46% of the vote and 58 of the 120 seats in the constituent assembly; the SOC's Cambodian People's Party received 38% and 51 seats; the remaining 16% went to smaller parties.

d) Promotion and Protection of Human Rights. The absence of a neutral political environment gave the human rights component a larger-than-expected responsibility for fostering a climate of confidence for the elections. The component rectified numerous instances of abuses, but remained powerless against systematic, orchestrated violations, such as Khmer Rouge massacres of ethnic Vietnamese and SOC murders of opposition leaders. It obtained the release of hundreds of political detainees and visited prisons to check treatment of the remaining prisoners. Conditions improved slightly, but hundreds remained detained without the prospect of a trial. The component also embarked on an extensive mass media campaign to explain notions of universal human rights. In conjunction with CIVPOL and the civil administration component, it ran education and training seminars for judges, defenders, police, and others in positions of responsibility.

e) The Repatriation Process. Despite dire prognostications from many refugee experts, the repatriation operation occurred smoothly. It began on March 30, 1992, with 526 Cambodians returning from Thailand and ended by March 1993, when the last camp in Thailand closed. Repatriation proceeded smoothly for several reasons -- UNHCR's lead time to prepare the process, as well as its large pre-existing presence in the region; the genuine wish of most Cambodians in Thailand to return; and, most important, the cooperation of all four factions with UNTAC and UNHCR. For the factions, repatriation not only did not threaten their vital interests, but the new arrivals represented potential sources of support.

f) Economic Rehabilitation. UNTAC's rehabilitation component coordinated foreign assistance for the reconstruction of the country; it had no budget of its own. The component assessed Cambodia's economic needs and developed a strategy for restoring the most pressing inadequacies in the country's infrastructure. Donors approached UNTAC with proposals, which then obtained the approval of a committee of the SNC to assure the factions that the funds would benefit the Cambodian people and not the SOC apparatus alone.

Despite the component's talented and dedicated staff, the realities of Cambodian politics sometimes overwhelmed it. For example, when UNTAC prepared the Secretary-General's April 19, 1992, appeal for international aid for Cambodia, it proposed using funds to finance the SOC's budget deficit (previously financed through printing of money). While perhaps prudent economics, the plan infuriated the resistance, who saw it as propping up the flailing SOC before elections. In addition, the component could not prevent some donors, such as Japan, from giving money directly to the SOC by bypassing the SNC.

g) The Education Function. UNTAC's Information and Education Division (not a component) provided critical assistance in the production and dissemination of information to Cambodians. It ran Radio UNTAC, developed video presentations, and printed and distributed numerous posters, leaflets, T-shirts and other trinkets on the elections and human rights. The Division's efforts constituted one of UNTAC's major successes, as it sought to convince Cambodians of the secrecy of their vote despite the violence and the omnipresent SOC. While the extent to which it succeeded in eliminating these fears will never be fully known, the high voter turnout is a testament to the Division's work. It also contained a small "analysis/assessment unit," a think-tank of Cambodia experts who travelled widely to gather intelligence on the plans of the factions and Cambodians' opinions about UNTAC.

3. UNTAC's Post-Electoral Functions

Although the successful election represented the culmination of most of UNTAC's work, the operation remained in the country for several more months, its numbers dwindling as personnel withdrew. UNTAC had two primary goals during this period. First, it assisted the Cambodian political leadership between the elections and the installation of a new government by attempting to build confidence among the winners and losers in the elections and assisting the constituent assembly in drafting the new constitution. Second, it arranged for a post-UNTAC UN office in Phnom Penh, headed by a UN representative, to coordinate the work of UN agencies in Cambodia.

Tackling UNTAC: A Model Operation?

Despite the many exogenous constraints on UNTAC, it was an independent actor during its 20 months in Cambodia; thus, the mission's operational competence and performance of its critical political functions require assessment.

1. Operational Competence

a) UNTAC's Understanding of Cambodia. While first-generation operations could undertake most of their duties with only military expertise, second-generation peacekeeping requires the integration of knowledge of the history, culture, and politics of the country. In this UNTAC proved only partly competent. First, it did not adequately teach its personnel about the historical struggle between Cambodia and its neighbors, the Khmer Rouge years, or Vietnam's invasion. Many in UNTAC saw the SOC only as saviors of Cambodia from genocide and were ready to blame the Khmer Rouge for all the country's difficulties or every violent episode, creating a perception of different standards of treatment for the SOC and Khmer Rouge. Compounding this trend, UNTAC did not effectively utilize the small reservoir of international experts on Cambodia -- expatriate Cambodians and a small number of scholars from academia, think-tanks, and governments -- only a handful of whom worked for UNTAC. Finally, although UNTAC could not expect its staff to speak fluent Khmer, it did not amply educate them about Cambodian culture and customs. On the seemingly mundane matters of politeness and ways to respond to disputes, most behaved well, but some, especially in CIVPOL, were ignorant of or flouted local mores.

b) Internal Management. As a multifaceted operation, UNTAC needed effective internal management. Akashi devoted little time to this question, and most decision making was organized only on a component-by-component basis, without sufficient procedures for the sharing of information and coordination of responses. The relationship among the components at the provincial level remained equally confusing, as officials had to refer disputes between components at the provincial level to UNTAC Headquarters.

UNTAC's relations with the international media that flocked to Cambodia for the mission also suffered. While the press acted on its instinct for hunting down negative stories, especially those involving casualties, Akashi and his staff did not use the press effectively. The press spokesman's temperament often antagonized journalists, and UNTAC only belatedly undertook an active effort to court the media to emphasize its accomplishments. Fortunately for UNTAC, the successful outcome of the elections became the media's final verdict on UNTAC, one the UN gladly embraced.

2. Political Performance

Like other second-generation missions, UNTAC had three core political functions -- administrator or executor of the peace accords, mediator of disputes, and guarantor of the result (in the modern, limited sense of that term). UNTAC had to implement its mandate despite the two main protagonists' refusal to cooperate and their accusations of bias. Its dilemmas in performing all three functions exceeded those in nearly all earlier missions.

a) The Special Representative of the Secretary-General. The greatest responsibility for carrying out these functions fell on Yasushi Akashi. While Akashi was politically acceptable for the job, possessed solid diplomatic skills, and had lengthy experience and knowledge of the UN, he lacked extensive familiarity with the recent politics of the conflict as well as significant international stature, which some saw as a source of UNTAC's difficulties. On the other hand, even a better candidate, such as Indonesian Foreign Minister Ali Alatas, a key broker of the Paris accords, might have achieved similar results.

Akashi came under intense criticism as politically unsophisticated by insiders and observers who claimed that his reliance upon the traditional Japanese search for consensus to overcome impasses hampered UNTAC's effectiveness. In fact, Akashi understood well the enormous job placed upon his shoulders and his different roles. He did adopt an approach that reflected his own background, a generally quiet, consensual-based manner to resolving disputes. Akashi thus very reluctantly asserted the full range of his authority under the Paris accords, especially with respect to binding directives and requests to remove or reassign personnel, and chose to act behind the scenes rather than use the media. Akashi saw himself as having only a finite reservoir of political goodwill with SOC leadership, which he had to utilize sparingly. Only in the five months before the electoral campaign did he deviate from this approach, as he reoriented the mission towards the election through, e.g. the deployment of the Control Teams.

Akashi thus sought his own balance between confrontation and conciliation. He clearly took his mediation roles very seriously, as he and his top aides negotiated indefatigably with the SOC over implementing UNTAC directives. At the same time, he maintained a clear vision of what he regarded as the one central mission of UNTAC -- the conduct of free and fair elections in May 1993. He rejected the advice of many in UNTAC who favored delaying the polling. Akashi's persistence created a goal and momentum, with UNTAC, as Akashi said in an interview with the author, as "custodians of the Paris accords."

Many found Akashi's approach skewed towards conciliation and compromise, and encouraged him to use his authority more freely. Some senior officials in UNTAC regretted that he did not use the removal power, UNTAC's key lever, more frequently and decisively. They believed this would have created the required fear in the minds of the SOC to pressure them into compliance with the civil administration control. These complaints, and the responses to them, highlight the possibility for different interpretations of the appropriate response for second-generation peacekeeping when consent erodes.

b) The World View of the UN Civil Servant. Akashi's preference for mediation over assertive executive action resonated clearly with UNTAC's career UN officials, who came from a tradition that places a premium on diplomatic discourse and proper relations with host authorities. UN civil servants in UNTAC's civil administration component took great pride in establishing friendly working relationships with SOC officials. This attitude, however, can entail significant costs in new peacekeeping operations. Recalcitrance by one party does not always, or even often, merit utilization of the traditional tools of the UN civil servant. Continually granting the violating side reprieves or seeking a compromise sends a signal to the uncooperative party that its behavior is costless.

The discord between this background and the demands of the new forms of peacekeeping left the UN bureaucrat unprepared for the control and direction required in the civil administration component. The lack of personal experience in governmental administration by most of these people compounded the effects of this predisposition. Instructions turned into requests, which evolved into favors, until the UN official interacted well with his SOC counterpart, who proceeded to ignore him. This pattern also affected perceptions of the operation's impartiality. Some opposition party officials, as well as the Khmer Rouge, feared UNTAC was too friendly towards the SOC because it regarded SOC as the *de facto* government to be salvaged in some way.

In addition, the various services and provincial directors within the civil administration component often did not seem to interpret their authority under the accords creatively enough. "Control" came to mean accomplishing a list of duties, or preparing a written directive, not imagining and taking whatever measures seemed necessary to effect a neutral political environment. Only late in the mandate period, when UNTAC established the control teams, did it fully use the accords as empowering instruments.

c) Contention in the Components. Not all members of UNTAC shared the perspectives of Akashi or the UN civil servants on the proper balance of mediation and execution. As a result, international civil servants and foreign officials seconded to UNTAC mistrusted each other in some ways. Career UN officials complained that outsiders lacked diplomatic skills and knowledge of the UN system, or tended to advance national goals. Those seconded to UNTAC noted the UN civil servant's penchant for avoiding confrontation, claimed they had a greater interest in career advancement than in the success of the operation, and found them lacking in necessary skills.

In addition, the different perspectives often divided along lines of nationality. The "Anglo" group - British, American, Canadian, Australian, New Zealander and southern African - dominated the human rights and electoral components due to their interest in and experience with these matters. They viewed the "Franco" group, which ran much of the civil administration component, as too timid to challenge the SOC. They accused the French of hoping that the SOC would win the election, thereby permitting the least disruption in Cambodia and advancing French interests in the region. The French group defined their approach as faithfully implementing the accords. They noted that quiet mediation would move the peace process along better than vocal objections. However, they believed UNTAC should have emphasized its executive role more with the Khmer Rouge. Each bloc thus argued that it favored confrontation over conciliation - but the Anglo group seemed to direct their policy more at the SOC, and the French at the Khmer Rouge.

These divisions manifested themselves in sharp differences among components over UNTAC's approach and priorities. The electoral component, with its plenary authority to organize an election notwithstanding the views of the factions, saw little need for compromise over the implementation of the Paris accords. The human rights component also emphasized strong measures against the SOC. They recognized that such action might cause the SOC to withhold cooperation from UNTAC on civil administration, but favored a principled approach despite the costs. If their efforts failed, they still held the moral high ground, with a clear conscience that they took all necessary steps against the violator of the accords. The civil administration component could not, however, afford to neglect the costs of punitive action, for the SOC still controlled the governmental apparatus. Harsh language and threats would not only not always accomplish UNTAC's ends, but might well undermine them. Each worked against the other through leaks to an eager foreign press.

The contentions within the components should serve as cautionary notices to those planning or assessing future second-generation operations. Different actors, and the same actors in different situations, can endorse contrasting, bona fide responses to challenges to impartiality and lack of consent, and the path to reconciliation of the various political roles. Moreover, simple chains of causation have little utility for evaluating the results of new peacekeeping operations. For each observer convinced that Akashi's consensual approach caused the Cambodians to lose respect for UNTAC, another can properly point out the consequences of alternative approaches. Each will draw contrary lessons of the best approach for new operations.

Criticism of UNTAC must be thus placed in perspective. As the largest peacekeeping operation since the Congo mission and the first with such a broad mandate, its *modus operandi* could not be expected to have satisfied all who worked in it, dealt with it, or observed it. It clearly could have done better operationally and politically, but it does not seem magnanimous to conclude that, on the whole, given the exogenous constraints, it capably carried out important parts of the UN's administrator, mediator, and guarantor functions.

The New Imperatives for the New Peacekeeping

The Cambodia operation and other recent missions suggest a number of priorities for the Organization and its members to make the new peacekeeping more effective. Most of the current public debate continues to emphasize the military side of the house, but long-term nation-building depends even more on the non-military aspects of peacekeeping.

1. Improvements to the Secretariat

a) Integration of Peacemaking and Peacekeeping. The inextricable link between peacekeeping and peacemaking must manifest itself in the UN's institutional readiness. Boutros-Ghali's important decision in 1992 to create a separate Department of Peacekeeping Operations (DPKO), along with the Department of Political Affairs (DPA), while responding to the growing number and complexity of peacekeeping operations, sacrificed the unity of peacemaking and peacekeeping within the Secretariat that prevailed for most of the UN's first 40 years. While DPKO and DPA should not be recombined, they must coordinate their activities more convincingly.

First, joint work must begin early in a peace process. Second, the Secretariat should expand its nascent practice of creating task forces across departments. Third, peacekeeping missions should include staff who participated in the peacemaking process. This may be difficult, as a Secretariat official may choose the conclusion of the settlement as a logical time to change jobs; or even undesirable, if an official has so antagonized the parties during the peacemaking stage as to be no longer regarded as impartial. In particular, the UN should start from the premise that a Special Representative who represents the Secretary-General before the signature of a peace accord will also do so after it.

b) Supervision of Non-Military Functions. The UN's current expertise in the military aspects of peacekeeping must be matched for the non-military aspects of new operations. In the case of UNTAC, for instance, only the electoral and repatriation components (in addition to the military force) had conducted detailed studies well in advance of UNTAC's arrival. The other components had to engage in on-the-job preparation that cost the mission valuable time.

Boutros-Ghali took an important step towards engendering institutional competence in non-military matters when he created the Electoral Assistance Unit within the Department of Political Affairs in 1992. This unit serves as a self-described "focal point" for all UN electoral assistance activities, from technical advice to a state to supervision of elections during a peacekeeping operation. The UN needs corresponding offices for civilian police, civil administration, human rights, economic rehabilitation, mine clearance, and possibly other subjects. Presently, specialized personnel are scattered in the United Nations Development Programme, the Centre for Human Rights, and elsewhere. These new units would be placed in DPKO and composed of a small number of experts to help plan operations and form liaisons with member states and other parts of the UN system. Boutros-Ghali's 1993 appointments of a senior police adviser and a de-mining expert are, thus, most welcome.

c) A Training Program in Non-Military Peacekeeping. Beyond establishing a formal planning mechanism at Headquarters, the UN must ensure that officials engaged in the new peacekeeping are competent for their new responsibilities. UNTAC demonstrated particular shortcomings in the areas of civilian police, civil administration, and human rights. Training thus becomes imperative for both international civil servants and individuals seconded from member states. The UN must form a pool of available civilian personnel ready for deployment in weeks, not months. The subjects for which preparation is required include public administration, human rights, basic economics, intelligence-gathering, politico-military expertise, and press relations.

One far-reaching method to accomplish this goal would entail the establishment of a full fledged training institute within the United Nations, akin to the United States Foreign Service Institute. The United Nations Institute for Training and Research (UNITAR) is not organized for this purpose; however, a revamped, reconstituted UNITAR or a new organization would train UN functionaries and officials from member states in the substantive work required for the new peacekeeping. It would graduate a new corps of UN reservists, each with a general background in all pertinent areas of peacekeeping and individual spheres of expertise. If this proved too expensive, the Secretariat could prepare courses to be taught by member states or private organizations. In addition, the UN should devise a short course for each operation, which all civilian members would attend. Finally, future leaders need to know how to manage an operation effectively. Some management training, perhaps by an outside consultant, should thus take place for senior officials who will form the pool of likely future Special Representatives.

d) Integration of Human Rights Awareness. If new peacekeeping operations continue to include human rights work in their mandates, the

United Nations will need to adjust its vision of the place of those rights in its agenda for peace. This problem calls for creating an institutional awareness about the centrality of human rights to the new peacekeeping. The UN already has an organizational basis for this greater consciousness, the Centre for Human Rights. The Centre cannot, however, ensure that key decision-makers incorporate human rights concerns, for its Geneva location puts it outside the mindset of those in New York working with the political organs on peacekeeping. The Centre had virtually no involvement in the planning of UNTAC.

e) Review of Procurement and Recruitment Practices. The significant number of civilians needed for UNTAC caught the UN unprepared; other operations have avoided this fate only because they had ample lead time (UNTAG had years to prepare) or smaller numbers of civilians (as with the electoral missions). The Secretariat thus needs to re-examine its ability to deploy people and supplies quickly for time-sensitive assignments. It should, especially, adopt procedures to facilitate waivers of competitive bidding, local procurement, and expedited recruitment.

f) Coordination with Specialized Agencies. To engage in nation-building through second-generation operations, the UN must draw upon people with technical skills to train and work with local personnel. The Congo mission broke new ground in this area in 1960; UNTAC engaged in this practice to a lesser extent, in its training of SOC officials in accounting and tax collection, and the use of the military component to train the post-election Cambodian army. The most available source of talent lies within the UN's specialized agencies, although member states may also be able to lend personnel quickly. DPKO should establish a coordination mechanism to involve them in new operations, including through secondment of personnel.

2. The Political Organs and UN Members

Improving the Secretariat's capacity to carry out the mandates handed it by the political organs represents a necessary, but not sufficient, step toward improving the new peacekeeping. The political organs and, through them, the member states, must share the onus of responsibility for these missions. While a certain disengagement by outside states from the settlement process seems inevitable once the Secretary-General assumes the primary mandate for running an operation, a major abnegation of accountability would be unwise. Oversight by the political organs indicates to the relevant elites in the target country that the international community retains an interest in their problem, provides a measure of support to the officials and staff of the missions, and affords member states control over the mission. Determining the type of oversight requires balancing the needs and desires of the member states to follow the settlement with the effects of supervision on the efficiency of the Secretariat and the operation.

a) Accurate Intelligence, Efficiency Shared. As a prerequisite to greater involvement, the Secretariat should provide a more candid account of the progress of operations than is often printed in the periodic reports of the Secretary-General. UNTAC's reports improved over time, candidly admitting the derailment of certain parts of the settlement and the hurdles to fair elections. Maintaining the perception of impartiality probably necessitates a cautious approach; nevertheless, the Secretariat should supplement its reports with frequent oral briefings. The Security Council could create formal subgroups to build upon the existing consultation between the Secretariat and interested members of the Council at the working level.

b) Principles of Oversight. Three power clusters -- the member states, the Secretary-General and his top aides, and the Special Representative -- have legitimate expectations that their views deserve deference, if not more, in the implementation of the mandate of an operation. To date, a *modus vivendi* has prevailed, with most authority exercised in the field. This outcome seems, however, to be as much the product of lack of resources and interest by the New York-based actors as a deliberate policy to afford flexibility to the field.

As a first principle, the political organs and Secretary-General should grant the Special Representative a wide berth in the internal management of the operation, such as selection of personnel, bureaucratic structure and decision-making, and requisition of equipment. With regard to the political responsibilities inherent in advancing the settlement process, the Special Representative should maintain significant discretion. Decisions to discuss implementation questions with representatives of political factions or to authorize components of the mission to undertake initiatives to advance the peace process should, in the first instance, require only an after-the-fact notification to Headquarters.

But the New York-based actors should assume the duty of overseeing the Special Representative more assertively regarding significant decisions. Two guiding criteria concerning the Special Representative's decision appear determinative of the desired degree of supervision by New York: (1) the risk of any decision derailing the successful completion for the mandate, and (2) the risk of any decision imperilling the safety of the personnel in the mission and the local population. As the aggregate of these two risks increase, the degree of oversight by New York should intensify. In some cases, the Special Representative need only notify Headquarters that he will execute a certain decision unless Headquarters objects, and an officer in DPKO, after consultations, can defer to him. More precarious moves, such as a decision to impose sanctions on a violating party, would require a formal request for permission, although exceptional emergency situations may preclude consultation.

3. Needed: A Review of Responses to Decaying Consent

Finally, the brief history of second-generation peacekeeping suggests that UN operations to implement settlements will face instances during their tenure of decaying consent, as one or more parties hesitate to carry out their obligations. The Cambodia experience reaffirmed that the ideal insurance against the worst manifestations of decaying consent is a demilitarized atmosphere. Yet missions will continue to occur in states with armed factions. Thus, once emplaced in such countries, the mission should attempt a demilitarization program as soon as possible, presumably in fulfillment of a peace plan.

Member states and Secretariat officials also need to evaluate the propriety of a more liberal or irrevocable view of consent for peacekeeping (not non-consensual enforcement) missions. This would entail encouraging future Special Representatives to make firm decisions about the implementation process and use diplomatic tools to convince the parties to comply with UN directives. If the parties do not comply with UN decisions within a reasonable period (a matter of days rather than weeks), officials in the operation should begin to attempt to correct the situation themselves, taking the parties at their word when they consented to the operation initially. Such a new policy would lead to a proper balance among the UN's executor, mediator, and guarantor roles. Where a settlement contains a clear obligation upon the parties, the UN's primary mission must be to assist the parties in fulfilling it. When legitimate interpretive disputes arrive, the UN can mediate, but if permitted under the accords, it must make the final authoritative determination. A philosophy that accepts violations of an accord as merely new issues for mediation entails few costs for the violator and pushes the parties back towards their pre-accord positions.

This new vantage point would pose risks, such as the possible transformation to peace enforcement, the potential for physical danger to UN personnel, and the damage to the credibility of the operation if a recalcitrant party continues to resist. Yet the use of firm measures within a consensual peacekeeping mission does not constitute, *ipso facto*, a step across the line to enforcement action; the earlier settlement agreed to by the parties affords the UN some leeway. The Council's support for UNTAC despite resistance by the two main factions -- including UNTAC's surprise raids on SOC offices and the conduct of the elections in the face of Khmer Rouge defiance -- suggests that the Council is accepting a broader notion of consent.

The hesitancy of the Secretary-General and member states to place peacekeeping personnel in harm's way is rational and inevitable. Yet the party opposing the UN's interpretation is likely to manifest its resistance through non-military means, as elevating opposition to the level of retaliation against UN personnel would invite universal condemnation. The Khmer Rouge's occasional attacks on UNTAC personnel elicited stern disapproval from its diplomatic allies and likely contributed to its decision not to disrupt the elections. If the UN's determination to carry out a directive did endanger UN personnel, the UN would clearly have to reassess before continuing. With respect to the credibility of the mission, a failed attempt to overcome an uncooperative faction will give rise to perceptions that the UN is a "paper tiger." Yet inaction in the face of such opposition can lead to the same conclusion more quickly.

A Final Word

This short paper has reviewed the performance of a mission that represented a qualitative change in the type of multi-functional operation the UN has undertaken. Its accomplishments and failures point to the complexity of determining the "success" and "lessons" of such missions, while nevertheless indicating clear areas for improvement. If these peace-implementation operations continue to proliferate, the UN's members must immediately devote sustained political, financial, and human resources to them.

SOMALIA: MAJOR ISSUES FOR FUTURE UN PEACEKEEPING

by Serge Lalande

The United Nations Peacekeeping Operation in Somalia (UNOSOM I and II) is a benchmark in the evolution of UN Peacekeeping[1]. UNOSOM is one of the largest UN peacekeeping operations, with more than 29,000 troops as of November 1993, supported by more than 17,000 US troops[2]. It is regarded as the first large-scale purely "humanitarian assistance" operation entrusted to peacekeeping, aimed at providing food and medical supplies to the starving Somali population. It was deployed amidst civil war, in a country with no government, where there was a proliferation of weapons and where armed gangs were looting food supplies that had became the Somali currency as well as the source of power and control over the population.

This operation, and its predecessor UNITAF, are perceived as a clear breakthrough in international humanitarian law because they constitute a classic case of humanitarian intervention in a country's internal affairs, under Chapter VII, to put an end to grave and massive violations of international humanitarian law[3]. This perceived breakthrough should,

[1] For a recent review and analysis of the UN operation in Somalia, see Makinda S. (1993), "*Seeking Peace from Chaos: Humanitarian Intervention in Somalia*", Occasional Paper Series, International Peace Academy, New York, 1993.

[2] UNOSOM II strength: 29,284 all ranks and approximately 17,700 US troops. S/26738, November 12, 1993, para. 47-48.

[3] See Roberts A. (1993), "Humanitarian War: Military Intervention and Human

D. Warner (ed.), New Dimensions of Peacekeeping, 69-99.
© 1995 *Kluwer Academic Publishers. Printed in the Netherlands.*

however, be tempered by the fact that, formally, it was a threat to international peace and security in the region that justified the intervention under Chapter VII, and the Security Council has recently insisted that it was the unique character of the absence of effective government that brought them into Somalia[4].

Another novelty is that this is the first time since the famous UN operation in the Congo that a peacekeeping operation has been deployed under Chapter VII with the right to use force and under the Secretary-General's command. It is also the first time, and perhaps the last, that the United States accepted putting American troops under UN command in a Chapter VII operation.

As a humanitarian relief operation, the UN intervention in Somalia is a positive achievement. The Somali population, thus far, is not starving anymore, for food production and the livestock sector have been reactivated. A large number of schools have reopened and children are being vaccinated. Furthermore, refugees and displaced persons are returning and the rehabilitation of the country's infrastructure has begun[5].

As a peacekeeping operation, however, its success is more mitigated, for UN peacekeeping in Somalia has encountered serious difficulties. Some of these, such as delays in the initial deployment and problems of logistics, of financing and of UN administrative procedures, are well known and have been acknowledged by the Secretary-General[6]. The solutions are also known and the situation might improve one day. Other problems, like UN unity-of-command, will certainly be discussed at length in the future.

Indeed, the deployment of such a peacekeeping operation under

Rights", *International Affairs*, Vol.69 No.3, July 1993, pp.429-450.

4 S/RES/794, December 3, 1992. S/RES/897, February 4, 1994.

5 S/26738, November 12, 1993, para.3-25 and S/1994/12, January 6, 1994, para.22.

6 S/26317, August 17, 1993, para.77.

Chapter VII has raised some major issues for the future evolution of United Nations peacekeeping operations. We will, therefore, concentrate our comments on the nature of the UNOSOM II operation in Somalia, on some aspects of its mandate and on some difficulties encountered in the progress of its mission, particularly those related to the June 5 attack against UNOSOM II personnel. But, first, we will look at the problems of the first peacekeeping operation deployed in Somalia.

Failure of UNOSOM I in Somalia: Inappropriate UN Reactions

UNOSOM I, perhaps along with the missions in Haiti and Angola, was certainly one of the worst experiences of United Nations peacekeeping operations in recent years. After months of delays in the face of an emergency situation, the UN deployed a peacekeeping force which proved unsuited to the circumstances, and the UN itself finally provoked an abrupt end to the mission by its decision to fire its Special Representative in Somalia, with far-reaching consequences for the future of UN humanitarian intervention in the country.

Because of its ad hoc functioning, the Security Council is ill-prepared to act effectively in a situation requiring its rapid intervention, with very harsh consequences for human suffering on the ground and a loss of United Nations credibility each time. Formally informed of the tragic situation prevailing in Somalia in January 1992[7], the Security Council started the long process of the deployment of a peacekeeping operation. In so doing, the Security Council was relying on the consent of the armed groups and was seeking to achieve exactly what had been tried

[7] Oral report by the Secretary-General, letter from the Chargé d'affaires (S/23445, January 20, 1992) and letters by regional organizations. See for instance S/23448, January 21, 1992. For a detailed description of the chaotic political, social, economic and humanitarian situation in Somalia, see the Consolidated inter-agency 90-day Plan of Action for Emergency Humanitarian Assistance to Somalia, S/23829, April 21, 1992.

previously, though unsuccessfully, by relief agencies; the problem was precisely that arrangements by the latter had proved ineffective[8].

The Security Council first requested the Secretary-General to promote a cease-fire[9], which came into effect on March 3, 1992[10]. A United Nations technical team was then sent to Somalia to organize the cease-fire monitoring mechanism and also to secure an agreement, concluded at the end of March[11], for the deployment of UNOSOM I[12]. The Security Council authorized the establishment of UNOSOM I on April 24, 1994, but in principle only, as the size of the force to be deployed remained to be negotiated with the two main factions in Mogadishu. It also approved the appointment of a Special Representative to direct UN activities in Somalia[13]. Ambassador Sahnoun was appointed on April 28, arrived in Mogadishu on May 4, and began his consultations with Somali leaders and other groups. The main factions in Mogadishu accepted the deployment of 50 military observers on June 25[14], but it was only on August 12, 1992 that an agreement was reached to deploy 500 Pakistani troops in Mogadishu. The UNOSOM force finally arrived in Somalia in September 1992. During this long process, the toll in human lives for the year 1992 was a staggering 400,000 as a result of this man-made

[8] S/23829, April 21, 1992.

[9] S/RES/733, January 23, 1992. The Security Council, considering that the continuation of the situation constitutes a threat to international peace and security, also decided, acting under Chapter VII, on a complete embargo on all deliveries of weapons and military equipment to Somalia.

[10] S/23829, April 21, 1992.

[11] S/23829, April 21, 1992.

[12] S/23693, March 11, 1992, approved by the Security Council on March 17, 1992, S/RES/746.

[13] S/RES/751, April 24, 1992.

[14] S/24179, June 25, 1992. The deployment was delayed because of an incident involving an aircraft chartered by WFP and said to be carrying Somali currency and military equipment for delivery to the Ali Mahdi faction in Mogadishu. S/24343, July 22, 1992.

famine[15].

UNOSOM troops spent most of the time stuck in their barracks and were totally unable to carry out their mandate[16]. In reality, the conditions necessary for the success of UNOSOM peacekeeping were not present at the time of its deployment, though this was foreseeable. First, the UN had secured a consensual agreement with the two major factions of Mogadishu, but not with the armed elements who were effectively controlling seaport and airport areas where UNOSOM was to be mainly deployed, and the UN knew that they were not under the control of the two factions[17]. Secondly, the peacekeeping force was to "provide convoys of relief supplies with a sufficiently strong military escort to deter attack and to fire effectively in self-defence if deterrence should not prove effective"[18]. In retrospect, 5,000 troops, instead of 500, would have been more likely to deter attacks at that time. In any case, lightly armed UN troops were neither in a position to deter any attacks nor to fire effectively in self-defence[19] against elements the UN knew were equipped with heavy weapons[20]. Sent "in conditions of continuing warfare"[21], without the consent of all parties and lightly armed to face

[15] Makinda, op.cit. note 1, p.43.

[16] See S/24859, November 27, 1992, for the difficulties encountered by UNOSOM.

[17] S/23693, March 11, 1992, para.11-40. S/23829, April 21, 1992, para.57. See also S/24343, July 22, 1992, para.54.

[18] S/23829, April 21, 1992, para.28.

[19] Such application of self-defence could also lead the peacekeeping force to become another warring party, at the risk of facing retaliation and losing cooperation on which it normally relies to succeed. See Liu, F.T. (1992), *UN Peace-keeping and the Non-Use of Force*, Occasional Papers Series, International Peace Academy, New York, 1992, and Goulding, Marrack (1993), The Evolution of United Nations Peacekeeping, *International Affairs*, Vol.69 No.3, July 1993, p.455.

[20] The defeat of the Somali army which, as a result of the Cold War, had become under Siad Barre one of the best equipped military machines in Africa, resulted in vast numbers of arms falling into the hands of individuals, factions and groups. S/24343, July 22, 1992, para.54. See also supra note 15.

[21] Goulding (1993) op.cit. note 19, p.458. Mr. Goulding proposes a typology of six different types of peacekeeping based on the functions performed by the

heavily armed groups, it is not suprising that UNOSOM encountered some difficulties.

However, the main reason for UNOSOM's failure was the loss, in October 1992, of the cooperation of at least one of the two main factions of Mogadishu, namely General Aidid's faction[22], following the firing of the Special Representative of the Secretary-General, Ambassador Sahnoun. Although the Secretary-General's reports are quite discreet on the events[23], the dismissal of Mr Sahnoun on October 26, 1992, for UN "domestic" reasons, seems to have been the turning point of the UNOSOM mission, and perhaps of the entire UN operation in Somalia[24]. Indeed, General Aidid, who was from the beginning very reluctant to have a UN presence in Somalia[25], had developed a special relationship with Mr. Sahnoun[26]. General Aidid apparently interpreted

peacekeepers. Somalia and Bosnia are classified under type Four "to protect the delivery of humanitarian relief supplies in conditions of continuing warfare".

22 S/24859, November 27, 1992. Fearing a forcible action by the UN, Ali Mahdi and General Aidid were reported to have made some moves towards a rapprochement against the "common enemy", i.e. the UN.

23 The following events are reported in a letter dated November 24, 1992 from the Secretary-General to the Security Council, S/24859, November 27, 1992.

24 Mr. Sahnoun publicly criticized the "nomenklatura" at UN headquarters and UN aid agencies' work in Somalia, criticism apparently deserved according to NGOs and some UN agencies. See for instance, "UN's Chief for Somalia Aid Resigns", *International Herald Tribune*, October 28, 1992; "The Squeezing of Sahnoun", *The Economist*, November 7, 1992; "M. Boutros-Ghali a accepté la démission du représentant spécial de l'ONU en Somalie", *Le Monde*, October 31, 1992. For an example of his comments, see "On peut éviter le recours à la force", *Le Monde*, August 10, 1992. See also Stevenson, Jonathan. "Hope Restored in Somalia?", *Foreign Policy*, No.91, Summer 1993, p.148, and Makinda (1993), op.cit. note 1, p.69.

25 See for instance, S/23693, March 11, 1992 and S/24343, July 22, 1992. Also Stevenson (1993), op.cit. note 24 on the accusation by Aidid that UNITAF was weakening him and fighting in Kismayu that angered Aidid against UNOSOM II (p.140-141). Moreover, Aidid had the impression that the UN was apparently tilting toward Ali Mahdi, and many Somalis see Boutros-Ghali as a Siad Barre during Boutros-Ghali's tenure as Egyptian Foreign Minister (p.149).

26 Stevenson (1993), op.cit. note 24, p.152. "By firing Sahnoun and enervating his

the firing of Mr Sahnoun as an indication of the UN's intention to resort to force and plan to invade the country. On October 28, 1992, he declared that UNOSOM would no longer be tolerated in Mogadishu, ordered the expulsion of the UNOSOM coordinator for humanitarian assistance, and warned that any forcible deployment of UNOSOM would be met by violence. The Secretary-General, trying to dispel these misperceptions, issued a statement that the purposes and methods of the United Nations under Mr. Kittani's leadership would remain unchanged. Nevertheless, it was too late, as apprehensions persisted. On November 12, General Aidid demanded the withdrawal of UNOSOM, which had at last succeeded in deploying at the airport[27]. On the Secretary-General's instructions, Mr. Kittani told General Aidid that the UN would not withdraw, and on November 13, the airport came under heavy fire by General Aidid's faction. By the end of the month, the Secretary-General and the Security Council concluded that it was necessary to review the basic premises and principles of the UN efforts in Somalia and found that the only option was to move into Chapter VII of the Charter[28].

The Secretary-General attributed the problems of UNOSOM to the size of the force and to a wrong mandate, and stated that the situation was not suitable for peacekeeping treatment[29]. In essence, a conventional peacekeeping operation was not the appropriate response to an emergency situation requiring the urgent delivery of humanitarian assistance in a country experiencing an ongoing civil war. Nevertheless, while Sahnoun's months of arduous and fruitful diplomacy had yielded positive results, his dismissal destroyed the fragile relationship built with

initiatives, the UN made a full-blown military occupation a practical necessity" (p.153).

[27] A few days before, UNOSOM had negotiated an arrangement with the airport security officials which was contested by Aidid, S/24859, November 27, 1992.

[28] S/24859, November 27, 1992 and S/24868, November 30, 1992.

[29] S/24868, November 30, 1992, S/24992, December 19, 1992 para 19. UNOSOM Force Commander General Shaheen also invoked the size of the force to explain their difficulties, "Commander Defends UN Role", *IHT*, January 25, 1993.

faction leaders and wasted these results.

THE PARADOXICAL NATURE OF UNOSOM II: A "NON-PEACEKEEPING OPERATION"

After UNOSOM I, UNITAF[30], the US-led operation, was authorized under Chapter VII to use force to establish a secure environment for humanitarian relief operations in Somalia[31]. It was obvious that UNITAF was not a peacekeeping operation. Nevertheless, its replacement, UNOSOM II, endowed with a stronger mandate and in essence the same objective, along with a few additional ones, is called a peacekeeping operation. The main distinction between UNITAF and UNOSOM II is that UNOSOM II is under UN command. Given this, does UNOSOM II really qualify as a peacekeeping operation? Or, are we witnessing the outset of a "third-generation" peacekeeping operation?

UNOSOM II is a coercive operation under Chapter VII of the Charter and is totally opposed to the notion of peacekeeping. Having two conflicting concepts under the same appellation of peacekeeping results in confusion, ambiguity, and uncertainty over future deployments of United Nations Peacekeeping Operations.

A peacekeeping operation is, from its origins, the antithesis of a military operation under Chapter VII. All the features of peacekeeping, namely consent of the State and of the parties involved, non-use of force except for self-defence, and neutrality and impartiality in the conflict, were designed to create a "non-army" and a "non-intervention force" in order to avoid the exclusive prerogatives of the Security Council under Chapter VII and to allow the General Assembly to deploy the first UN peacekeeping force in Egypt in 1956[32]. In contrast, UNOSOM II is

[30] Unified Task Force, also known as Operation Restore Hope.

[31] S/RES/794, December 3, 1992.

[32] See *The Blue Helmets*, United Nations, New York, 1990, p.43-78.

deployed without the consent of the parties, has the right to use all necessary measures to carry out its mandate -- including the right to the use of force -- and, far from being neutral towards the parties, UNOSOM II, on the contrary, runs the risk of having to fight them if it is necessary to put an end to what is considered a threat to international peace and security. If a peacekeeping operation is, by definition, a "non-Chapter VII operation", UNOSOM II, deployed under Chapter VII, is a "non-peacekeeping operation".

In his proposal for the deployment of UNITAF, later approved by the Security Council[33], the Secretary-General stated that UNITAF would be replaced by a conventional peacekeeping force as soon as a secure environment was provided by UNITAF throughout Somalia[34]. But, as we shall discuss later, no such secure environment was achieved, even according to the Secretary-General[35]. In addition, the US argued that a force mandated and organized on normal peacekeeping lines would not be capable of protecting humanitarian activities from factional forces or gangs which would not have been neutralised or disarmed during the presence of UNITAF in Somalia. The US envisaged UNITAF's replacement by a new UNOSOM which would be under UN command-and-control but whose mandate, concept of operations, levels of armament and rules of engagement would be little different from those of the UNITAF itself. The Secretary-General then underlined that such a force would differ from the peacekeeping model and would constitute the first peace-enforcement operation to be carried out under UN command[36]. However, instead of proposing a remodelling of UNITAF,

[33] S/24868, November 30, 1992, 4th option. S/RES/794, December 3, 1992.

[34] S/24868, November 30, 1992.

[35] S/25354, March 3, 1993, para.58. S/24992, December 19, 1992, para.26.

[36] S/24992, December 19, 1992, para. 38-41-43. The Secretary-General also stressed that this approach would be analogous to the fifth option he favored in his letter in November (S/24868, November 30, 1992). Note that the United Nations Operation in the Congo (ONUC) was the first UN chapter VII operation under the Secretary-General Dag Hammarskjöld's command. See *The Blue Helmets*, op.cit.

a kind of UNITAF II, or another name for the new UN peace-enforcement operation, the Secretary-General opted for an enlargement of the UNOSOM peacekeeping operation and a redefinition of its mandate to include operations under Chapter VII[37].

Several consequences ensue from the enlargement of a peacekeeping operation to a "peace-enforcement/peacekeeping operation", some of which could have a negative impact on the future of UN peacekeeping operations.

First, the acceptance of the deployment of a United Nations peacekeeping operation by the host State and the warring parties to a conflict could prove more difficult in the future. This may be so if the operation is perceived as liable to be transformed into a peace-enforcement operation against one party which initially accepted its deployment, simply because the Security Council is not satisfied with the implementation of its resolutions or with the way the parties are complying with their own agreement.

Second, for the States contributing troops, the move into a coercive operation could prove more difficult to reconcile with their values or their constitutions, as in the case of neutral countries such as Austria, Finland, Sweden or Switzerland[38], or for countries like Canada and the Nordic countries, or for countries with constitutional restrictions on foreign military involvement, like Japan and Germany.

Third, another major consideration for contributing States in the transition from a peacekeeping operation to a UN peace-enforcement action is that the decision to get their country involved in what could be a war requires a totally different political analysis of both their domestic

pp.213-260.

37 S/25354, March 3, 1993, para.56. "The consequence of such a decision would be far-reaching for political, legal and logistical reasons and would entail a major financial commitment". No elaboration of the consequences followed.

38 By a popular initiative, a referendum will be held in June 1994 in order to decide whether or not Switzerland should contribute troops to UN peacekeeping operations. *Journal de Genève*, February 25, 1993.

and foreign policies prior to committing troops. There is a great difference between the political decision to help a country, at the latter's request, to restore law and order, and the political decision, even for humanitarian purposes, to intervene in the internal affairs of another country to impose Security Council decisions by force. Such an intervention would normally be justified only if a country's strategic national interests are involved.

Fourth, in military terms, a peacekeeping operation differs substantially from a peace-enforcement operation. In the former, the Force Commander never takes the initiative in using force and tries to de-escalate the level of tensions at each incident. In the latter, the Force Commander must conduct offensive operations to achieve specific military objectives as efficiently as possible. Also, whereas peacekeeping relies on the host State for the infrastructure of the operation, using communications, transportation, energy, lodging, supplies and all other facilities that might be available in the country, a peace-enforcement operation cannot depend on any help from within the country to perform its mandate. Because the mission is riskier for the personnel, the chain-of-command and unity of command must be tighter in a coercive operation than in a peacekeeping operation; therefore, a peace-enforcement mission would be more efficient with a smaller number of States contributing troops than would be a peacekeeping operation, which favors involving a larger number of countries. While the contingents should be chosen from countries neutral to the conflict, the peace-enforcement operation is likely to find its troops in countries which have sufficient national interest, troops and military equipment to impose the decisions of the Security Council in the designated country. Furthermore, the role of the peacekeeper, who has changed from aggressive to pacific behavior, must once again revert to that of a combatant.

Fifth, the relations with the parties are also totally different. From a relationship of cooperation and confidence, as the peacekeeping operation acts as a neutral third party, we move to an adversarial relationship, with the peace-enforcement mission in a position of authority.

With the enlargement of UNOSOM I to UNOSOM II, the distinction between these two opposed types of operations is obfuscated, and even disappears. Such an amalgam of conflicting concepts might lead to confusion, uncertainty and ambiguity in the minds of policy makers currently designing the shape of their countries' involvement in future peacekeeping operations, as in the United States, Japan, Germany and Switzerland. Finally, the lack of a clear-cut distinction between an operation relying on the consent of the parties and a coercive peace-enforcement operation renders it virtually impossible for UN Member States, the press, and the world as well as national public opinion, to understand the role, nature, and purposes of future UN peacekeeping operations.

It would have been possible to consider this operation as an exception, as was the Congo operation, since the Secretary-General and the Security Council have underlined the unique character of the operation in Somalia[39]. However, following the Security Council's reflections on *An Agenda for Peace*, this uncertainty and ambiguity about the nature of a peacekeeping operation became embedded in "UN Peacekeeping Operational Guiding Principles" adopted by the Council in May 1993. Under these principles, largely influenced by the UN missions in Somalia and Bosnia[40], the consent of the government is required, "save in exceptional cases", as well as the consent of the parties concerned "where appropriate", and only the Security Council itself can put an end to an operation, not the parties. The Security Council asserts its "readiness to take appropriate measures against the parties which do not observe its decisions" and the "right of the Security Council to authorize all means necessary for United Nations forces to carry out their mandate". Impartiality is no longer in relation to the parties or the conflict but "in implementing Security Council decisions"[41]. Such

39 S/25354, March 3, 1993, para.100.

40 And probably to a certain degree by the missions in Cambodia and Angola.

41 S/25859, May 28, 1993.

principles allow the Security Council, and its peacekeeping force, to cross the frontier from a consensual to a coercive operation, from an operation which serves the parties to one which imposes the will of the Security Council on them. Perhaps the General Assembly's Special Committee on peacekeeping operations[42], responsible for determining guiding principles for UN peacekeeping operations, could examine the implications of this Security Council statement.

MAJOR ISSUES RAISED BY UNOSOM'S II MANDATE

1. Peacemaking and Peace-enforcement: Incompatible Mandates

UNOSOM II has been endowed with a much broader mandate than UNITAF[43], since it is involved in all "peace" activities possible for a UN operation throughout Somalia[44]. In addition to *a peace-enforcement* capability, UNOSOM II is responsible for several standard *peacekeeping* activities such as cease-fire monitoring, demining[45], assistance in the repatriation of refugees[46] and displaced persons, and, less frequently,

[42] The Special Committee on Peace-keeping Operations, also called Committee of 34, was created on February 18, 1965 by the General Assembly's resolution 2006 (XIX). For the last report of the Committee, see A/48/173, May 25, 1993.

[43] S/RES/814, March 26, 1993, referring also to the Secretary-General's report S/25354, March 3, 1993, para.56-88.

[44] UNITAF activities had covered only 40% of the territory (S/25354, March 3, 1993, para.6). UNOSOM II is deployed over 100% of Somalia, including in the self-proclaimed republic of Somaliland. The UN denied recognition to Somaliland, leaving to the political process the decision on the constitutional arrangements with Somaliland (S/25354, March 3, 1993, para.98) and in the same way has refused to withdraw UN troops from their territory at the Somaliland "President's" request (S/26526 and S/26527, October 1, 1993).

[45] Somalia is one of the 10 most heavily mined countries in the world (S/26738, November 12, 1993, para.45).

[46] 300,000 refugees, according to UNHCR figures (S/25354, March 3, 1993, para.25).

implementation of the arms embargo[47]. UNOSOM II is also entrusted with elements of *post-conflict peace-building* activities. It is empowered to provide assistance to the Somali people in rebuilding their social and political life, rehabilitating the country's economy, infrastructure and institutions and re-establishing a neutral civilian police force and judicial system[48]. In addition, UNOSOM II is entrusted with high-level *peace-making* activities - to organize, promote and advance a political settlement and national reconciliation through broad participation of the people of Somalia.

However, the association within UNOSOM II of peace-making functions and peace-enforcement duties appears to be incompatible with and counterproductive to UN efforts to achieve a political settlement between the two main factions. It is, indeed, very difficult for UNOSOM II to act as an impartial third party to help the parties reach an agreement while at the same time using force against one of them.

Actually, one cannot deny the achievements of the Special Representative and the political affairs component of UNOSOM II, which were not really covered by the media[49]. They effectively brought about broad participation of Somalis in the national reconciliation process by inviting participants representing political movements; civic, community, religious and women's groups; NGOs; and elders and eminent persons.

[47] Very little has been done to implement the Chapter VII arms embargo (S/RES/733, January 22, 1992). The Secretary-General repeatedly reported that arms were continuing to flow into Somalia (for instance, S/23829, April 21, 1992 and S/24343, July 1, 1992, para.53).

[48] The Security Council requested the Secretary-General to submit a report as soon as possible containing recommendations for the establishement of Somali police forces (S/RES/814, March 26, 1993, para.18). However, it was only on August 17, 1993 that the report was submitted (S/26317, August 17, 1993, Annex 1) and it was approved by the Security Council on September 22, 1993 (S/RES/865, September 22, 1993).

[49] The Secretary-General has acknowledged that the public information activities tried to foster greater awareness of these activities, but without great success (S/26317, August 17, 1993, para.53).

They have also succeeded in helping to resolve regional conflicts and intercommunal disputes[50]. Moreover, they have contributed to the implemention of the March 1993 Addis-Ababa agreement providing for the establishment of district and regional councils that could eventually lead to the establishment of the Transitional National Council which would rule Somalia during the transitional period[51].

However, despite these positive developments, the peace process through UNOSOM II remains deadlocked[52]. Two obstacles continue to impede progress: deep divisions between the main factional alliances and the continued rejection by SNA (General Aidid's faction) of all political initiatives undertaken by UNOSOM II. Discussions have bogged down over the issue of whether or not the UN should play a role in the national reconciliation process, and the SNA has alleged that UNOSOM II encouraged the other party to exclude the SNA from the national reconciliation process. In his January 1994 report, the Secretary-General states that "UNOSOM II does not and will not take sides among various factions... It is only SNA which has a negative, even hostile, attitude towards UNOSOM II"[53]. This does not take into account the search for General Aidid by UNOSOM II during the summer of 1993, the air strikes against his headquarters, Radio Mogadishu and his weapons and ammunition storage sites, and the arrest of his supporters. All these factors make it very unlikely that UNOSOM II will ever succeed in bringing the parties to a peace settlement and make it understandable that Aidid no longer considers UNOSOM II as an impartial mediator.

[50] S/26317, August 17, 1993, para.23 and 40.

[51] 53 out 81 district Councils (excluding the north-west region "Somaliland") and 8 out of 13 regional Councils have been established as of January 1994 (S/1994/12, January 6, 1994, para.9-13).

[52] S/1994/12, January 6, 1994, para.3. Some progress was reported recently toward agreement on forming a Somali Government, after talks in which US special envoy is acting as go-between. *IHT*, February 5, 1994.

[53] S/1994/12, January 6, 1994, para.3-6 and 49.

2. Enforced Disarmament of Factions: The Hidden Political Agenda

One major element of the initial mandate of UNOSOM II was to disarm armed gangs and irregular forces, movements and factions in order to create a "secure environment" for humanitarian assistance in Somalia[54]. According to the Secretary-General, UNITAF was supposed to provide Somalia with such a "secure environment", which should have included complete disarmament throughout Somalia[55]. However, the US-led operation limited its action to the minimum necessary to secure relief supplies and achieved very little disarmament[56]. Consequently, the Secretary-General proposed a mandate to disarm all unauthorized armed elements and to bring under international control the heavy weapons of the organized factions[57].

Nobody challenged that part of the mandate. The disarmament was necessary to establish law and order and peace and stability on a lasting basis, which would provide for a secure environment for humanitarian assistance and would also be necessary to achieve national reconciliation and all other elements of UNOSOM II's mandate[58]. While the

[54] S/RES/814, March 26, 1993.

[55] The Security Council resolution (S/RES/794, December 3, 1992) endorsed the recommendation by the Secretary-General (S/24868, November 30, 1992) that action under Chapter VII should be taken in order to establish a secure environment by disarming armed gangs and factions (para.7) and welcomed the offer by a Member State to establish an operation to create *such* a secure environment (para.8).

[56] See the Secretary-General report S/24992, December 19, 1992, para.19 ss. Far from disarming, UNITAF advance parties announced the arrival of UNITAF forces so that fighters and weapons were barely visible upon their entry into a new area (S/25126, January 19 1993).

[57] S/25354, March 3, 1993, para. 57 c) and d). At the time of UNOSOM I, the faction leaders and clan elders were asking the UN to disarm the population and irregular forces, but not the factions (S/24343, July 22, 1992, para.65). It was only after the attack against UNOSOM I at the airport in November 1992 that the Secretary-General started to talk about neutralizing the heavy weapons of organized factions.

[58] S/26317, August 17, 1993, para.14-73.

disarmament of armed gangs and irregular forces was already a rather ambitious objective in a situation of proliferation of arms throughout Somalia, the seizing of the heavy weapons of the organized factions would be an even more difficult step since it represents a substantial undertaking for military personnel.

However, disarmament of organized factions is not just a question of law and order and peace and stability. In reality, UNOSOM II has received a mandate which would, in essence, change the political landscape of Somalia by modifying the relative positions of the political factions in the country. To do so on the basis of an agreement among the parties themselves is not a problem. However, although the Secretary-General has recommended that the disarmament process should be carried out under the modalities agreed upon by the Somalis themselves in the Addis-Ababa agreement[59], under the supervision and with the cooperation of UNOSOM II, he did not change the nature of the operation in order to rely on consent and cooperation of the parties. Instead, he has proposed that disarmament, to be effective, should be enforceable. It would also be continuous and irreversible, lasting as long as required or until a Somali government was functioning effectively, and conducted simultaneously throughout Somalia[60].

UN peacekeeping has very little experience in disarmament. In

[59] In January 1993, the parties agreed that all heavy weaponry would be handed over to a cease-fire monitoring group, the militias of all political movements would be encamped and disarmed simultaneously throughout Somalia and all other elements, including bandits, would be disarmed immediately (S/25168, January 26, 1993, Annex III). It is not clear to what extent Genral Aidid gave his consent to the March 1993 agreement. The Secretary-General reported that "the Somali parties themselves had anticipated that the disarmament might not proceed smoothly and that some form of coercive action might become unavoidable" (S/26738 November 12, 1993, para.84). "[Disarmament was indispensable and was] recognized by virtually all Somalis, including the leaders of political factions who agreed in Addis Ababa in January and March to such disarming and urged UNOSOM II to apply strong and effective sanctions against those responsible for any violation of the cease-fire agreement of January 1993" (S/26317, August 17, 1993, para.14).

[60] S/25354, March 3, 1993, para.61-64.

interstate peacekeeping operations involving sovereign States, the UN never had to disarm the parties. In intrastate peacekeeping operations, the UN has experience in disarming factions in Cambodia, El Salvador, Angola and Mozambique.

Disarmament is always a very critical political process and probably the most delicate phase of any peace-building operation. In the process of disarmament, the faction leaders are asked to give up their military power, the main source of control and political authority in a civil war situation, in exchange for a chance to participate in a future political process which might give them a role in the future government of the country.

Disarmament is a loss of power. If this is achieved prior to a global peace agreement, it leads to a major change in the respective bargaining power of the parties in negotiations on their role in the future government. By disarming the strongest party, a political advantage is thus given to the weaker parties[61]. Moreover, in contrast to an interstate peacekeeping operation, in intrastate situations it is the political survival of the leaders themselves which is at stake. Understandably, it is the leader who relies the most on military power to exert his influence over the country who is the most likely to resist surrendering military power and to seek guarantees that his political durability and comparable power for himself will be ensured through the political process. These faction leaders will normally accept such a shift of conflict from the military arena to the political arena only within a global peace agreement where every part is closely interconnected with the others and which will protect their interests at each phase of the peace process.

Even then, we have seen how delicate and difficult is the implementation of such agreements. In Cambodia, the Khmer Rouge

[61] That is why, from the beginning, Ali Mahdi faction was supporting UN peacekeeping. See for instance S/23693, March 11, 1992, para.35 and S/24343, July 22, 1992, para.13. See also Stevenson (1993), op.cit. note 24, p.146: "Because they [Ali Mahdi faction] were militarily weaker than Aidid, they favored UN intervention as an equalizer".

refused to disarm, arguing, among other things, that one crucial part of the agreement concerning the control over the Phnom Penh Government by UNTAC had not been implemented[62]. In El Salvador, ONUSAL had to readjust the timetable three times for the disarmament of the parties in order to respect the built-in equilibrium of the peace agreements[63]. In Angola, UNITA had resisted disarming to the point that only 25% of its disarmament was completed by the time the elections were held[64]. In Mozambique, it took one year to reach an agreement on the implementation of a global peace agreement, with RENAMO, for example, asking that they be accorded enough money for their election campaign before they began the disarmament process[65].

The disarmament of political factions is a costly political undertaking that can take place only through a global peace agreement and with the cooperation of the parties, especially the one relying the most on its military power. Failing such cooperation, implementation by coercion is unrealistic for a UN force. Imagine the difficulties the UN would have faced trying to disarm by force the Khmer Rouge in Cambodia, Savimbi in Angola, or RENAMO in Mozambique. Nevertheless, it is precisely this impossible mandate that was given to UNOSOM II, which tried unsuccessfully to implement it.

From the beginning, the Secretary-General was conscious of the adverse political effect of the UN's action on the influence of faction leaders[66]. He was also aware that "disarmament must not destabilize the security balance and must equitably reduce the threat to all segments of

62 S/24090, June 12, 1992 and S/24286, July 14, 1992.

63 S/24833, November 23, 1992.

64 S/24556, September 9, 1992.

65 S/26034, June 30, 1993.

66 "UNITAF's presence has reduced the influence of those whose power was based on their heavy weapons" (S/25354, March 3, 1993, para.6). "The priority that UNOSOM II gave to disarmament has generated the hostility of a few clan leaders, fearful of losing their power, towards UNOSOM" (S/26317, August 17, 1993, para.72).

the population"[67]. However, in the aftermath of the June 5 attack against its personnel, UNOSOM II undertook a series of actions to restore security and law and order by implementing a comprehensive program for disarmament in Mogadishu, or more precisely, in South Mogadishu. Far from simultaneous disarmament of all political factions, the UN action aimed at neutralizing heavy weapons and command and control facilities of the strongest faction in Somalia, General Aidid's faction[68]. Subsequently, UNOSOM II and the US entered into war with him. After unsuccessful attempts to arrest Aidid and to control South Mogadishu, and after the killing of 18 US Rangers on October 3, 1993, the UN was forced to give up. In January 1994, the Secretary-General reported that "UNOSOM II tried to bring about disarmament through coercive means. However, as the members of the Security Council are aware, this course of action has proved to be impracticable"[69]. Since that failure, the major factions are now reportedly rearming in anticipation of a return to widespread fighting after the withdrawal of US troops on March 31, 1994[70], nullifying previous efforts at disarmament.

3. Excessive Use of Force by UNOSOM II: Empowered for Warfare or Police Action ?

The main events related to the use of force by UNOSOM II occurred in the aftermath of the June 5 attack against UNOSOM II personnel and the killing of 25 Pakistani troops ambushed presumably by supporters of General Aidid's faction. In the following weeks and during the summer of 1993, UNOSOM II and the US Quick Reaction Force conducted a series of attacks against Aidid's faction during which a large number of

[67] S/26738, November 12, 1993, para.84.

[68] S/26022, July 1, 1993, para.17-19 and 40.

[69] S/1994/12, para.32.

[70] S/26738, November 12, 1993, para.37 and S/1994/12, para.34.

Somali civilians were killed. UNOSOM II has been sharply criticized for excessive use of force in violation of human rights, international humanitarian law, and the United Nations' own basic standards[71].

The day after the June 5 attack against UNOSOM II, the Security Council requested the Secretary-General to inquire into the incident, with particular emphasis on the role of those factional leaders involved, reaffirmed that UNOSOM II was authorized to take all necessary measures against those responsible for the armed attacks, and re-emphasized the crucial importance of the early implementation of the disarmament of all Somali parties as well as of neutralizing radio broadcasting systems that contribute to the violence and attacks against UNOSOM II[72].

Between June 12 and June 25 1993, UNOSOM II undertook a program[73] to restore security and law and order in Mogadishu, by implementing a comprehensive program for disarmament, neutralizing broadcasting systems, and searching, clearing and disarming the Aidid headquarters area in South Mogadishu. To achieve these objectives, UNOSOM II conducted a series of precision air strikes and ground military actions. These strikes were carried out "utilizing tactics that would *minimize* Somali casualties as well as collateral damages to nearby areas" and "to allow those in the stronghold to depart" in the case of the attack on Aidid's headquarters. The broadcast studio of Radio Mogadishu in downtown Mogadishu "was disabled by precision air attack in the

[71] For instance, see *Peace-keeping and Human Rights*, Amnesty International, London, January 1994, AI Index IOR 40/01/94. "Several hundred Somalis, including many women and children have been killed, as have over 60 UN troops and 18 US soldiers. Some of the civilians killed by UN or US troops seem to have been victims of the use of lethal force in breach of human rights and international law obligations" (p.18). "As has already happened in Somalia, such a response may involve the disproportionate and excessive use of force, in contravention of international standards guiding law enforcement personnel" (p.28).

[72] S/RES/837, June 6, 1993, para.3, 5 and 6.

[73] All the events described below are reported in S/26022, July 1, 1993, para.17-19-20-23-25 and 45.

early morning when minimally occupied. UNOSOM II reported that this timing avoided the military and civilian casualties that would have resulted from a ground assault to seize the facility"[74]. In demonstrations against UNOSOM II, civilian crowds, including women and children, were used by General Aidid and his supporters as human shields to screen attacks on UNOSOM II forces. On June 13, shots were fired from the crowd at UN soldiers on the ground and a UN soldier on a rooftop returned fire[75]. Moreover, according to the UN, armed Somalis nearby also fired at the crowd to make it appear as if UNOSOM II had fired at the crowd. The number of Aidid's supporters and Somali civilians killed by the UN during these attacks and all other attacks was not reported by the UN. Media reports suggest that at least several hundred Somalis were killed[76].

The nature of UN actions was militarily justified, even at the risk of killing Somali civilians, by the military objectives. Leaving aside the question of whether, under the circumstances, such actions constituted excessive and disproportionate use of force and indiscriminate attacks prohibited under international humanitarian law[77], and the question of whether the UN force is subject to the laws of war, the main issue raised here is how UNOSOM II should have exercised its right to use force and, more specifically, whether this should have been used as in a warfare situation or as in a police action.

UNOSOM II is an intrastate operation. Because of the absence of effective government in the country, UNOSOM II was sent under Chapter VII of the Charter to exercise supreme authority in Somalia,

[74] Note that the timing of the morning attack is opposed to a ground assault instead of an afternoon attack, and the reasons for the choice of an air strike are not precisely explained.

[75] Killing at least 20 people, *The Economist*, June 19, 1993 and *IHT*, June 16, 1993.

[76] For instance, "but the relentless hunt for the General has killed at least 500 Somalis". "Manhunt", *The Economist*, September 18, 1993.

[77] See Amnesty International, op.cit. note 71, p.32.

being empowered, at least for the objectives set in its mandate, as the unique source of legal coercion within the country. UNOSOM II was sent with a mandate to restore law and order, to re-establish the Somali police force, to work for national reconciliation and re-creation of a Somali State based on democratic governance, and to replace the lawless rule of guns prevailing in the country by the rule of law. Such a mandate entails a UN peace-enforcement mission of a purely intrastate nature, acting like a good government would, in accordance with the highest standards promoted by the UN within the international community of States[78]. In consequence, as for any other State based on democratic principles and respect for human rights and the rule of law, the appropriate course of action for UNOSOM II in dealing with illegal actions, notwithstanding their gravity, is to act and react as in a police action[79]. Even if military personnel are required to perform the tasks, this does not change the essential nature of the operation as a police action[80].

Leaving aside the paradoxical situation in Mogadishu of trying to minimize civilian casualties while carrying out indiscriminate air strikes, it is obvious that such air strikes, even precision air strikes, are not in conformity with police action by a good government. Under the terms of the Security Council resolution, UNOSOM II was authorized to take all necessary measures against those responsible for the armed attacks, including the investigation of their actions and their arrest and detention for prosecution, trial and punishment[81]. In the context of police action, "necessary measures" would normally suggest that force should be used

[78] Amnesty International proposes a list of standards that should apply to UN peacekeeping operations. Amnesty International, op.cit. note 71, p.45.

[79] According to the Secretary-General, the nature of the mission in Somalia is one of a police action. UNITAF was a short-term police action (S/25354, March 3, 1993, para.90). He also stated that successful police and justice systems would also render the UN military presence no longer necessary (S/26317, August 17, 1993, para.69).

[80] See also Amnesty International, op.cit. note 71, p.27.

[81] S/RES/837, June 6, 1993, para.5.

only if there are no less harmful options, and that only the minimum and proportionate force necessary should be used[82]. In addition, while civilian casualties may be inevitable in war despite restrictions imposed by international humanitarian law, in police action, civilian lives must not be put at risk, save in exceptional circumstances.

The reaction of the UN to the attack against its forces sparked a guerrilla-type war in Mogadishu, with UNOSOM II becoming a new warring party in the civil war, which was contrary to its mandate to restore law and order in the country. Moreover, these attacks by UNOSOM II were in retaliation for the premeditated killing of UNOSOM II soldiers on June 5, 1993. The severity of the attacks against Aidid's premises and supporters, the use of air strikes on his headquarters and weapons storage sites, the focus on the disarmament of his faction only, and the neutralization of his propaganda instrument, Radio Mogadishu, provide abundant indications that the UN sought retaliation for the June 5 attack, which is behavior unsuitable for a police action. Even though retaliation was not the formal mandate of UNOSOM II under the Security Council resolution, the Council has nevertheless supported such action by UNOSOM II[83]. The Secretary-General later confirmed that UNOSOM II should be given the means to retaliate against attacks on its personnel[84]. One has to question whether retaliation is one of the

[82] Amnesty International refers to international human rights and criminal justice standards such as the Code of Conduct for Law Enforcement Officials (A/RES/34/169 of December 17, 1979) and the Basic Principles on the Use of Force and Firearms by Law Enforcement Officials (adopted in September 1990 by the 8th UN Congress on the Prevention of Crime and the Treatment of Offenders,Havana, Cuba). Amnesty International op.cit. note 71, p.31.

[83] Overall, the resolution supported such action. It also urged "Member States to contribute on an emergency basis military support and transportation, including armoured personnel carriers, tanks and attack helicopters to provide UNOSOM to confront and deter armed attacks against it". The Security Council further requested the Secretary-General to submit a report on the implementation of the resolution, if possible, within seven days from the date of its adoption. (S/RES/837, June 6, 1993).

[84] "UNOSOM II must retain capability for coercive disarmament and *retaliation*

standards promoted by the United Nations among its Member States.

Two considerations might contribute to explaining the use of air strikes. First, the US, entrusted with the command of the Quick Reaction Force, has a tendency to favor an overwhelming force that will ensure a rapid victory and to favor the use of the most sophisticated military technology in order to minimize their own casualties. The second, a cause of the first, is the desire to avoid the erosion of American public support which might have occurred if US soldiers were killed, and which could have provoked the withdrawal of American troops from Somalia[85].

Ensuring the rule of law would also have required the setting up of an effective and impartial judicial system for enforcement of the law by UNOSOM II. However, no such system was put in place until the end of 1993[86]. In the meantime, Somali detainees were held in UN custody without being charged with any offense, without access to relatives or lawyers[87] and without being brought before any court. This situation in a police action, as opposed to military practices in a war or civil war situation, amounts to arbitrary and indefinite detention without charge or trial, in contravention of the UN's own human rights standards[88].

An impartial investigation of alleged violations of humanitarian law should have been conducted on both sides since UNOSOM II was also involved in shooting at civilians. However, while UNOSOM II was retaliating against Aidid's faction, the Secretary-General appointed an American to conduct an impartial investigation of the June 5 attack against UNOSOM II. Even if the person appointed was capable of being impartial, any appearance of impartiality was mitigated by the fact that he was an American designated by UNOSOM II, itself headed by an

against attacks on its personnel" (S/26738, November 12, 1993, para.91.).

85 "Le représentant de l'ONU justifie le recours à la force", *Le Monde*, July 15, 1993.

86 S/1994/12, January 6, 1994, para.17.

87 Although ICRC delegates have been allowed to visit them.

88 Amnesty International, op.cit. p.20.

American, and by the fact that UNOSOM II, through its retaliation against Aidid's faction, had already deemed Aidid guilty. Actually, the Security Council implicitly accepted this argument with the creation in November 1993 of a Commission of Inquiry to investigate the same events[89].

4. Violations of Humanitarian Law by General Aidid's Faction: The Search for a Criminal or for a Political Leader?

For any political authority facing illegal or criminal activities by political movements pursuing political objectives, it is always problematic to know whether to approach these events as criminal offenses by calling for consistent judicial treatment for the individuals responsible, or as the manifestation of community issues requiring a political solution, or both. Such a dilemma is never easy to solve. To some extent, UNOSOM II was in a similar situation following the June 5 attack by General Aidid's faction against UNOSOM II, considered by the UN a grave violation of international humanitarian law.

The UN decision was to treat the events at several levels. At the individual level, a total of 740 Somalis were arrested[90] and a warrant (which proved unsuccessful) was issued for the arrest of their leader, General Aidid. It is on the grounds of "mounting evidence" that the UN has decided that Aidid was personally responsible for the attack[91]. Furthermore, the UN undertook the disarmament of Aidid's faction.

For General Aidid, the June 5 attack was a clear challenge to the UN's authority to disarm his faction and to stop his propaganda[92]. For

[89] S/RES/885, November 16, 1993. See also the letter of the Organization of African Unity (S/26627, October 25, 1993).

[90] S/26738, November 12, 1993, para.74.

[91] S/26022, July 1, 1993, para.32-33.

[92] Aidid's perception was that UNOSOM II intended to seize his Radio Mogadishu. (S/26022, July 1, 1993, para.5).

its part, UNOSOM II interpreted the general's actions as seeking confrontation in order to take control of the political reconciliation process[93]. UNOSOM II saw the June 5 attack as a declaration of war, a struggle for power between UNOSOM II and General Aidid's faction[94]. And, indeed, this is what it became.

In the face of this political challenge to the UN's authority and its mandate in Somalia, UNOSOM II sent a written message to General Aidid advising him that this was the last opportunity for him to become part of the peace process[95]. There were no direct talks with General Aidid, no serious evaluation of his demands, and no attempt by UNOSOM II to try to restore the peace process by diplomatic means. Instead, UNOSOM II entered into war with his faction, and lost. While crimes are acts of individuals, the collective actions of UNOSOM II against the whole faction of General Aidid transformed what the UN was calling a criminal case into a political struggle for power. As a result, UNOSOM II had to withdraw its warrant for Aidid's arrest, free his supporters, and stop its coercive action and disarmament in Mogadishu[96].

This is not to say that the UN should not have taken action against violations of humanitarian law and human rights. The UN cannot remain silent in the face of such violations in accordance with its own standards. Should a political movement be involved in criminal offenses, the appropriate police action for the UN - if it is to act like a good government in a State where the rule of law prevails - is an individual

[93] S/26022, July 1, 1993, para.12. General Aidid in a personal broadcast over Radio Mogadishu articulated more anti-UNOSOM II rhetoric, urged calm if UNOSOM II acquiesced to his demands, and violence if it did not. Aidid's demands are not indicated in the Secretary-General's report.

[94] S/26022, July 1, 1993, para.42. "The priority that UNOSOM gave to disarmament generated the hostility of a few clan leaders, fearful of losing their power towards UNOSOM" (S/26317, August 17, 1993, para.72).

[95] S/26022, July 1, 1993, para.13.

[96] S/26738, November 12, 1993, para.98.

approach against the persons responsible, provided that they are given a truly impartial investigation and a fair trial. In the meantime, as in any democratic society, political talks with political leaders are the normal way to settle political issues, which was Aidid's challenge to the UN's authority.

CONCLUSION

The 50th anniversary of the United Nations could be the opportunity for the UN, its Member States, and the Security Council to review the instruments of collective security and of promotion of peace and stability and to reassess their guiding principles. The UN missions in Somalia have highlighted significant elements for that purpose. In discussions concerning the future evolution of United Nations peacekeeping, three considerations should be borne in mind.

First, UN peacekeeping, especially since 1989, has evolved from interstate to intrastate operations endowed with prerogatives and functions of governments, as in the operations in Cambodia, Mozambique and Somalia. However, intrastate peacekeeping operations are not considered differently and their functions are performed under the same guiding principles of consent, non-use of force and impartiality as interstate operations. The missions in Somalia have revealed the necessity for the UN to adopt additional principles consistent with the intrastate nature of such operations.

We have mentioned that the UN is legally bound to the standards of conduct it promotes within the international community of States. However, it is the whole peacekeeping philosophy which needs to be adapted to the particular intrastate character. Interstate peacekeeping operations are state-centric and imbued with military doctrine inherited from the first generation of peacekeeping operations. Intrastate peacekeeping, in accordance with the democratic principles of the

Universal Declaration of Human Rights[97], should be people-centric. This "democratization" of the intrastate peacekeeping missions would entail rethinking and reorienting all aspects of the operation at all stages of its organization and deployment.

For instance, military personnel could be replaced by police officers with the support of a special military unit for more demanding tasks. Civilian units more oriented towards peace-building activities and conflict resolution at the ground level could contribute more to restoring peace after a civil war or ethnic conflict than the strict and necessary institutional approach to peace-building. An important human rights component is as important as judicial organs in creating a state governed by the rule of law. In order to develop closer links with the population for whom strictly such a mission is deployed, a consultative body composed of eminent persons without any political allegiance could be put in place at the very beginning of the mission to serve in an advisory capacity to reflect the opinion of the population. For the transitional period, peaceful-settlement-of-disputes mechanisms can be set up in order to remove obstacles to an irreversible process towards a lasting peace.

Second, in this era of concern for ecology and the environment, one might admonish others to "save the peacekeeping species". UN peacekeeping is a "truly UN" creation[98]. UN peacekeeping has, over the years, built a strong reputation for genuine impartiality which was guaranteed by the consensus necessary for the deployment of peacekeeping operations in the context of the antagonist-veto system prevailing in the Security Council during the Cold War.

The amalgam of "peacekeeping/peace-enforcement" operations should not become the third, and thus unique, generation of UN peacekeeping operations. There are many reasons for a clear-cut separation of the two types of operations: the potential irreversible loss of impartiality, the

[97] In particular, article 21, para.3 "The will of the people shall be the basis of the authority of the government".

[98] "United Nationsness", as Mr. Goulding puts it, op.cit., note 1, p.454.

absence of continuity in the transition from one to the other in terms of military units, military equipment and logistics, rules of engagement and mindsets of the soldiers, unity-of-command, size of the force, and, more importantly, the different national interests involved for countries contributing troops which necessitates new political decisions. Furthermore, warring parties are more likely to accept the deployment of peacekeeping as a confidence building measure if the Security Council avoids blending its role of promotion of peace and stability at the service of the parties with its duties as guardian of international peace and security under Chapter VII of the Charter.

If the Security Council attempted to deploy a UN conventional peacekeeping force in Somalia in 1992, and subsequently deployed a UN peace-enforcement operation under the peacekeeping name, it is for the simple reason that peacekeeping is the sole existing instrument available to the Security Council for UN interventions on the ground. Therefore, it is time for the UN to create a distinct UN peace-enforcement unit. Had such an instrument existed at the time of UNISOM I, the Secretary-General might never have proposed an enlargement of UNOSOM I to UNOSOM II.

Third, UNOSOM I and II and UNITAF have demonstrated that when aid agencies' attempts to provide assistance are impeded due to warfare conditions in a country, the humanitarian assistance operation requires the Security Council to resort to forcible action under Chapter VII of the Charter. Here again, the need is obvious for a ready-to-deploy peace-enforcement unit, which might accelerate the ad hoc intervention of the Security Council in an urgent situation. Had such an instrument existed, the Secretary-General might never have proposed the unsuccessful deployment of UNOSOM I.

However, the US intervention and withdrawal under media-influenced public opinion and, to a certain degree, the recent difficulties of the Secretary-General in recruiting new contingents have proven that altruistic humanitarian assistance does not constitute sufficient national interest for any lasting involvement of UN Member States. In order to escape this lack of interest among individual countries to intervene when the international community has a clear interest to do so, such an enforcement unit should be composed of non-nationals and be deployed solely under the UN flag.

Keynote Address

A JAPANESE PERSPECTIVE ON PEACEKEEPING

by Hisashi Owada

THE PLACE OF PEACEKEEPING IN A NEW INTERNATIONAL ENVIRONMENT

It has become something of a truism that the international order is undergoing a historic transformation. As a starting point for our discussion, however, it is important to be clear about the essential nature of this transformation and to assess its impact upon the structure of international order. The demise of the structure of Cold War confrontation, resulting from the collapse of the Soviet Empire, came about largely because the Soviet system could not cope with the contradictions between the social reality of interdependence within the international community and the systematic rigidity of the socialist regime in its political, economic and social manifestations. This has brought about a new situation, for the first time since the end of the Second World War, where an international order based on *pax consortis* is the order of the day.

This transformation is most clearly illustrated by the coordinated international response, as led by the United Nations, to the crisis in the Gulf. As is well-known, the crisis was triggered by an act of outright aggression by Iraq against Kuwait, a fellow member of the United Nations, in blatant violation of the most fundamental norms of international law as enshrined in the UN Charter. A series of subsequent developments have abundantly demonstrated that in this new environment

D. Warner (ed.), New Dimensions of Peacekeeping, 103-116.
© 1995 *Kluwer Academic Publishers. Printed in the Netherlands.*

the international order has to be maintained through cooperative efforts of major players. As a nucleus of the new international order, the United Nations has an important -- indeed critical -- role to play as an organization with primary responsibility for the maintenance of peace with justice in the world.

Under such circumstances, the international community has increasingly come to expect the United Nations to take greater initiative in the maintenance of peace and security. The Security Council has responded to this challenge by launching a number of peacekeeping operations to contain and resolve conflicts. Indeed, the peacekeeping operation has now become a major field of UN activity.

Some of these peacekeeping operations, such as the United Nations Transitional Authority in Cambodia (UNTAC) and the United Nations Transition Assistance Group in Namibia (UNTAG), have been extraordinarily successful. Others, such as UNPROFOR in former Yugoslavia and UNOSOM in Somalia, have revealed that there is a serious gap between the expectations of the international community for peacekeeping operations and the capacity of the United Nations, as supported by the political commitment of its members, to carry them out with success. Thus it has come to be widely acknowledged that, in light of these experiences of more recent years, it is time to review and re-examine the whole institution of peacekeeping operations with its basic assumptions.

In order to clarify the nature of the problems that are now confronting UN peacekeeping operations and to explore the implications of those problems for future UN peacekeeping operations, it is necessary to analyze in some detail the present state of peacekeeping operations as currently conceived.

The increased demand for peacekeeping operations since the end of the Cold War has resulted in their quantitative and qualitative expansion. Suffice it to refer to some figures to illustrate the quantitative expansion of peacekeeping operations. Of all the operations launched in the history of the United Nations, two-thirds of them, or 20 out of 33, have been established since 1988; six were established in 1993 alone. By the end of 1993 the number of personnel engaged in these operations had increased to approximately 70,000. The number of personnel engaged in a single operation has also increased. UNTAC, UNPROFOR and UNOSOM II, for example, have each engaged more than 20,000 personnel. As one might imagine, the financial requirements have also increased dramatically. Indeed, the budget for peacekeeping operations in 1993 is estimated to be over US $3 billion, which is approximately three times the size of the regular UN budget.

Traditionally, the primary purpose of peacekeeping operations has been to prevent the recurrence and aggravation of conflicts by intervening between the conflicting parties. The United Nations Truce Supervision Organization (UNTSO) in Jerusalem, the United Nations Disengagement Observer Force (UNDOF) in the Golan Heights, the United Nations Military Observer Group in India and Pakistan (UNMOGIP) and the United Nations Peacekeeping Force in Cyprus (UNFYCIP) are examples of this type of relatively small-scale operation.

Since towards the end of the 1980's, by comparison, peacekeeping operations have come to be regarded more as part of the global peace process. Some of them have been entrusted with an essentially civilian task of overseeing the establishment of a new government through a national election. These operations include a wide range of activities such as election monitoring, human rights monitoring, refugee repatriation, and national reconstruction and rehabilitation. The operations launched in Namibia, Cambodia and, most recently, Mozambique have included, at least in part, an operation of this type.

THE EVOLUTION OF JAPAN'S POLICY ON PEACEKEEPING

It was against the background of such evolution of the peacekeeping operations of the United Nations that Japan came to feel it should be able to contribute more actively to the peacekeeping operation of the United

Nations within its existing constitutional framework. Thus Japan decided in 1990 to embark upon a somewhat ambitious task of creating a new legal framework for cooperating with the United Nations in its peacekeeping activities.

The 1947 Constitution of Japan, which deeply reflected the national sentiment of the Japanese people after the experience of the Second World War, declares that "the Japanese people forever renounce war as a sovereign right of the nation and the threat or use of force as means of settling international disputes," that "in order to accomplish (this) aim, land, sea and air forces, as well as other war potential, will never be maintained" and that "the right of belligerency of the state will not be recognized." While Japan was admitted to the United Nations in 1956, for many years it has carefully chosen not to get involved in a peacekeeping operation of the United Nations by way of physical participation in the form of its national contingent.

With the evolution and expansion of the peacekeeping activities of the United Nations in recent years extending to the areas of election monitoring, refugee repatriation and other civilian missions, however, Japan gradually started to involve itself little by little in those new areas of peacekeeping operations of a civilian type, where no domestic political controversy relating to the constitutional constraint could arise, while an overwhelming bulk of Japan's contribution to the peacekeeping operations of the United Nations remained basically in the realm of financial contributions to bear the costs of operations carried out by other national contingents. As a background to this, there was a prevailing national sentiment, almost amounting to a national psyche, that Japan should not get involved in any conflictual situation even vicariously and that the dispatch overseas of her Self-Defense Force should never be considered for any purposes.

It was the Gulf Crisis of 1990-1991 which sent a shockwave through this national psyche and triggered the process of exposing the Japanese people to the new reality of the world for the first time since the end of the Second World War. The impact of the Gulf Crisis was serious enough to let the people of Japan come out of their psychological cocoon which had isolated them from the reality of the outside world throughout these years after the end of the War. People were confronted with harsh criticism addressed to Japan by some allies for "being too slow in offering too little" in its cooperation with the international community for its fight against the blatant aggression by Iraq. In fact, people in Japan were initially somewhat perplexed by the absence of proper appreciation in the international community for its enormous financial contribution amounting to US $13 billion, painfully extracted from the people by way of a new special tax. Through this painful experience, people in Japan for the first time came to be awakened to the importance of sharing the burden by shedding blood, sweat and tears, if necessary, and not just money, as a responsible member of the international community fighting in common for the maintenance of peace with justice.

It was against such a background that the Government embarked upon a new attempt to prepare a legal framework for enabling Japan to participate more actively in the peacekeeping efforts of the international community. What turned out to be a major obstacle in this process was the issue of whether Japan should participate in the multilateral forces deployed in the Gulf region. This issue became a subject of intense debate. The original draft for a proposed new legislation as prepared by the Government would have enabled Japan to send military personnel to the Gulf as part of the multilateral forces. This, however, did not gain support in the Diet, as it rekindled the old debate on the constitutionality of Japan's Self Defense Force itself and particularly its dispatch overseas. The cardinal issue focused on was whether members of the Self-Defense Force could be utilized, even in a supportive capacity, for activities of a multilateral force which, strictly speaking, was not under UN command. Nevertheless, public support for creating a new legal framework for enabling Japan to participate in a joint action by the international community for a common cause gained ground. As a result of agonizing reappraisal of the experience of the Gulf Crisis, the Government proposed in September 1991 a new draft of the legislation which would allow the dispatch of a Self-Defense Force to those peacekeeping operations that are under UN command. Given the essentially controversial nature of the issue, however, a major compromise had to be struck among the political parties in the process of passing the new law through the Diet; the law as finally adopted would empower the Government to send military personnel to participate in the logistical sides of peacekeeping activities only, while holding in abeyance the dispatch of contingents to participate in a full-fledged peacekeeping operation going beyond logistical activities by stipulating that this part of the law shall not be implemented until a further date to be set forth by another new legislation.

Not only is the new law somewhat restrictive in its scope in this sense, but it is also contingent upon five conditions that must be met before Japanese forces can be dispatched. The five conditions are the following:

1) a cease-fire must be in place;
2) the parties to the conflict must have given their consent to the operation;
3) the activities must be conducted in a strictly impartial manner;
4) participation can be suspended or terminated if any of the above conditions is not met; and
5) participants may not use weapons except in self-defense *stricto sensu*, i.e. in cases where a member of the Japanese contingent is personally attacked.

Be that as it may, the International Peace Cooperation Law, as the new law is called, has established for the first time in the postwar history of Japan a legal framework which enables Japan to participate in UN peacekeeping operations and international humanitarian relief activities. Since its enactment in 1992, Japan has already dispatched personnel to Angola and Mozambique as part of the contingents for UN peacekeeping operations and is preparing to send 15 election monitoring officials to El Salvador in March 1994. It has also contributed to the peace process in

Cambodia by dispatching altogether 1,200 members of its Self-Defense Force to participate in major UN efforts there. This was the first time since the end of the Second World War that Japanese troops were sent overseas.

New Problems of Peacekeeping in a New Setting

The demise of an international order based on the bipolar confrontation has brought about the eruption to the surface of many local conflicts based on ethnic, religious or hegemonic motives, as well as the collapse of Government structures in a situation of civil strife. All these new developments, which had hitherto been contained within the structure of the Cold War confrontation, have brought about a totally new picture, requiring a fresh new look for the role of the United Nations in its peacekeeping activities to cope with this new situation, side by side with the traditional peacekeeping activities of the United Nations which remain important.

Against the background of this newly emerging environment of the post-Cold War world, Secretary-General Boutros-Ghali has taken a new initiative to cope with this new situation, directing his attention to the development of a new type of operation. This includes, *inter alia*, a new operation whose task it is to secure the safety of personnel engaged in humanitarian relief operations conducted in areas where a cease-fire is in danger of collapsing. UNPROFOR in the former Yugoslavia and UNOSOM II in Somalia are two examples of operations entrusted with such a mandate. Another new type of operation, which the Secretary-General has proposed in his *Agenda for Peace*, is one to be deployed for the purpose of preventing the outbreak of a conflict. The operation established in the former Yugoslav Republic of Macedonia in 1993 is the first example of such an operation.

This expansion of peacekeeping operations has created a host of serious problems in such areas as the procurement of personnel, financing, and the security of personnel. Indeed, unless the problem of insufficient resources is squarely addressed, it is feared that another large-scale operation may not be possible. As regards personnel, whereas there was at one time a ready supply of forces to serve in infantry battalions, this is no longer the case. The idea of creating a stand-by force as put forth by the Secretary-General is an attempt to cope with this problem.

Even more acute is the difficulty in the procurement of financial resources besetting the United Nations. The Secretary-General has felt compelled to make a personal appeal directly to the leaders of individual nations to pay the amount of their assessed contributions in arrears, which as of the end of 1993 has reached approximately US $1 billion.

It is submitted that recent experiences of the United Nations in its peacekeeping operations have provided us with some important points to reflect upon from the viewpoint of how the peacekeeping operations of the United Nations should be conducted in the new setting. Here, an attempt is made to depict some of the more salient points as concisely as possible.

The first and perhaps the most important point to reflect on is the problem of how, in what way and to what extent the United Nations should become involved in a situation where there is a civil war and where the country's central authority has collapsed, in particular in relation to the task of providing humanitarian assistance. The position of the United Nations on this problem has not always been sufficiently clear, to say the least. As a result of this lack of a clear mandate, the operation of peacekeeping has sometimes become overburdened. Its experience in Somalia is a case in point.

In particular, as peacekeeping operations expand their scope so that they engage in activities to secure compliance with requirements for humanitarian purposes, there arises a dilemma between the principle of impartiality inherent in the traditional peacekeeping operation and the need for imposing an element of enforcement in the situation. The element of enforcement involved will almost inevitably bring about a situation where the United Nations will risk becoming to that extent a party to the conflict, as the experience of Somalia has taught us. This is an extremely delicate point that requires sober reflection, since the principle of impartiality is particularly important if future peacekeeping operations are to be successful in the traditional context.

The second and equally important point to keep in mind is the problem of co-relationship between the operation in peacekeeping and the overall process for political settlement. The traditional peacekeeping operation to prevent the recurrence or aggravation of a conflict by intervening between the disputing parties has a better chance to succeed in bringing about a durable peace when conducted in the context of a parallel political process for peace. The Cambodian operation is an exemplary case in this sense, in that it demonstrated that a peacekeeping operation, carried out in the context of an overall peace process conducted through closely coordinated diplomatic efforts, can achieve remarkable results within a defined time frame.

It should also be remembered in this connection that when peacekeeping activities are undertaken as part of such a comprehensive peace process, their success depends to a great extent on the political will for peace of the parties concerned.

The third point which merits our attention is the problem of preventive deployment. This new device has already been put to the test of practice with some measurable success in the operation in Macedonia. The validity of this new device has been affirmed in a General Assembly resolution. The problem that confronts us is how we further explore and test this in other potentially dangerous areas, to the extent that it offers a promising fertile ground for the future development of peacekeeping activities of the United Nations.

Finally, another problem which is of critical importance to the viability of the UN peacekeeping operation in the future is the problem of safety of personnel engaged in UN operations.

The qualitative expansion of peacekeeping operations has meant that personnel engaged in such activities are often placed in vulnerable situations and must often discharge their responsibilities in the face of extreme danger. The number of casualties incurred during these operations has increased rapidly: 59 personnel engaged in UNPROFOR and 81 in UNISOM II have been killed in the short space of time these operations have been under way. As a result, some countries have already withdrawn their troops form these operations; others are expected to do so in the near future. This situation has very serious implications for the future of peacekeeping operations as a whole. The current effort of the United Nations to address this problem by considering the possibility of enacting an international convention for the security of personnel is an eloquent testimony to the seriousness of this problem.

In relation to all these new problems confronting the peacekeeping operation, the Secretary-General has offered several important suggestions in his report *An Agenda for Peace*. This report has been discussed in a wide range of forums, including the Security Council, General Assembly, and the Committee on Peacekeeping Operations. Based on a sober reflection on these discussions, a few personal thoughts are hereby offered as to how these difficult problems might be addressed.

First, let us start with one area where a new approach to the UN peacekeeping operation has given rise to a delicate problem, i.e. the problem of protection for humanitarian activities. When the authority of a central government has completely collapsed and competing factions within the country are engaging in acts of violence, a peacekeeping force is required to ensure that humanitarian assistance is delivered to those for whom it is destined. Under these special circumstances the concept of peace enforcement as proposed by the Secretary-General would seem to have certain validity. At the same time, the lessons gained through the experience in Somalia have taught the Security Council to be cautious in invoking the provisions of Chapter 7 of the UN Charter for launching a new type of peacekeeping operation for this purpose. Any enforcement action should be carefully planned, in which the time-tested principle of impartiality should be carefully weighed against the need for taking an action containing an element of enforcement so that peacekeepers may not become victim to the conflict themselves. It would seem useful in this connection to engage in an exercise in post-mortem of the operation in Somalia in order to ascertain how the outcome of the operation could have been different if the operation had been conducted in a more cautious way and in a less peremptory manner, thus avoiding the risk of antagonizing the local population.

Second, with regard to the problem of co-relationship between the peacekeeping operation in a situation of military conflict and the overall process for political settlement, the successful conclusion of the Cambodian operation provides a valuable lesson. The secret of the success in Cambodia, it is submitted, lay in its comprehensive and multifaceted approach. Because the situation in Cambodia was extremely complex, it would have been futile to attempt to succeed in its peacekeeping goal simply by deploying a traditional peacekeeping force there. Intense diplomatic efforts, in which Japan together with other like-minded countries played a decisive role in close coordination with the permanent members of the Security Council, succeeded in bringing about a degree of national reconciliation which enabled the framework established under the Paris Agreement to function for the restoration of peace in Cambodia. UNTAC was then established with a mandate that included a wide range of tasks, from the organization and conduct of free and fair elections to civil administration. UNTAC itself involved some 22,000 personnel and was the costliest operation ever launched by the United Nations, but what was equally important was that parallel with that the countries concerned were engaged in a concerted diplomatic action for creating a political environment conducive to durable peace, together with the offer of economic assistance which laid the groundwork for an economic recovery plan once the elections were held. This well-planned operation should serve as a model for future UN efforts.

It bears repeating that as the Cambodian experience so clearly demonstrates, the political will of the parties involved and the comprehensive planning of an operation are the two factors that are most essential to the success of an operation.

Third, the importance of preventive diplomacy can not be overemphasized. History has taught us the tragic lesson that the restoration of peace, once a conflict has already broken out, entails tremendous efforts and costs in terms of human and material resources. As was indicated earlier, the UN deployment of troops in Macedonia as a means of preventing the conflict in former Yugoslavia from spilling across the border has proved highly successful. This deployment of forces for preventive purposes has enhanced Macedonia's sense of security. It is true that at its inception the underlying concept was a subject of intense discussion at the United Nations, but finally in the recent session of the General Assembly consensus has been reached on its realization. The potential of preventive deployment should be more fully utilized in situations that are likely to threaten international peace and security. In the same vein, sending UN investigation missions to areas where there is the danger of eruption of a conflict can be extremely useful as an exercise in preventive diplomacy.

Last, the safety of personnel engaging in UN operations is a serious problem which could affect the future of peacekeeping operations of the United Nations. On the basis of the discussions held in the Security Council and the General Assembly and the report issued by the Secretary-General last August on this score, a couple of suggestions may be in order:

1) It seems desirable that the activities of the Office of Security Coordinator at Headquarters to be strengthened. A fresh effort should be made to achieve a degree of integration and accountability among various bodies to ensure the security of UN personnel. Expert staff should be recruited to assist the Security Coordinator and his designated officials in the field.
2) Whenever the Security Council discusses a peacekeeping operation, it should take into consideration the security of personnel involved. Moreover, it is the responsibility of the Secretariat to inform the members of the Council as to whether the Secretary-General has been

given sufficient means and resources to protect the lives of those who are engaged in the peacekeeping operation in question.

By way of a summing up of this chapter, it should be emphasized that, with respect to all these problems that the United Nations is confronted with in the new situation, the maintenance of informal consultations among the Secretariat, the contributing countries, and the members of the Security Council are of essential importance. In view of the complexity of large-scale operations that are envisaged, a mechanism of this kind needs to be established in order to make the contribution of considerable financial and human resources by member countries easier and the whole peacekeeping operation more acceptable to the member countries by involving them in a consultation process. This idea was received with little enthusiasm when Japan first proposed it several years ago, but it would appear that the proposal has come to gain greater support from many countries in recent years. In fact, it has since been incorporated in some recent General Assembly resolutions. It should be pointed out that the mechanism for consultation among countries concerned has greatly contributed to the success of the Cambodian operation. In view of the increasing complexity of UN peacekeeping operations, the Security Council cannot be expected to bear the burden alone; elaboration of a mechanism of this kind should be seriously considered.

CONCLUSION

In an age when the international community is at a historic turning point and is in search of a new order, the role to be played by the United Nations has grown dramatically. In this regard, in particular, special attention is focused on strengthening the peacekeeping functions of the United Nations. In Japan also, a soul-searching debate has now started, in an effort to find an answer to the question as to what constructive roles and responsibilities Japan should carry out in this regard.

As has been mentioned earlier, Japan has established the legal framework which enables her nationals, including members of her Self-Defense Force, to participate in some of the UN peacekeeping operations. Moreover, as the scope of peacekeeping activities of the United Nations expands to cover areas relating to civil administration as an important element in UN operations, Japan will be able to contribute more actively through participation in these new areas by civilians.

Although the new legislation places certain limitations on the participation of military personnel from Japan at present, it is believed a consensus is growing rapidly that Japan should play a more prominent role for the world, including more active participation in the peacekeeping activities of the United Nations. The day should not be too far ahead when the Japanese participants will be more visible in different parts of the world, engaging in peacekeeping activities of the United Nations, in cooperation with other countries that have gained broad experience and know-how in this area.

Special Address

THE INTERFACE BETWEEN PEACEKEEPING AND HUMANITARIAN ACTION

by Sadako Ogata

Some traditional peacekeeping operations in the past have contained humanitarian elements, notably the Congo. But, by and large, during the Cold War political and humanitarian actions were seen as distinctly separate, however untenable or unreal that division might have been. With the proliferation of internal conflicts and humanitarian crises in the post-Cold War world, and with a much greater willingness on the part of the international community to address them, that relationship has undergone a metamorphosis.

I would like to examine the implications of this complex relationship from the perspective of a humanitarian organization. I will analyze some specific cases to illustrate the limits and prospects of cooperation between the humanitarian and the politico-military components of the United Nations. Finally, I would like to draw some conclusions about how to improve that cooperation, while safeguarding the specificity, neutrality and impartiality of humanitarian action.

Let me begin by briefly describing the background to the growing prominence of humanitarian issues on the international political and security agenda.

The end of the Cold War has unleashed, and in some cases intensified, internal conflicts, particularly ethnic ones, on a scale rarely seen before. Massive population displacement is a direct consequence, and sometimes, as in the former Yugoslavia and Georgia, the very objective of the conflict. In the past two years, UNHCR has had to respond to several

D. Warner (ed.), New Dimensions of Peacekeeping, 119-127.
© 1995 *Kluwer Academic Publishers. Printed in the Netherlands.*

major humanitarian emergencies, at least three of them affecting over a million persons. In April 1991, 1.7 million Iraqi Kurds fled to Iran or the Turkish border. UNHCR is assisting over a million Somali refugees in the neighboring countries of Kenya, Yemen, Djibouti and Ethiopia. In the former Yugoslavia, we are protecting and assisting over 1.5 million refugees in Serbia, Croatia and Montenegro as well as almost 3 million displaced and affected population in Bosnia and Herzegovina. Last November, in the space of one fortnight, some 600,000 persons fled ethnic killing in Burundi to seek refuge in Rwanda, Tanzania and Zaire.

In addition to almost 20 million refugees and other persons assisted by UNHCR, there is probably an equal, if not greater, number of internally displaced persons in refugee-like conditions. Although UNHCR does not have a general mandate for this group of persons, at the request of the Secretary-General we are protecting and assisting the internally displaced of Bosnia and Herzegovina, Armenia, Azerbaijan, Tajikistan and Sri Lanka. Our action on behalf of the internally displaced has been encouraged and endorsed by the UN General Assembly, particularly when there is a link to an existing or potential refugee problem.

UNHCR's growing involvement with the internally displaced persons is both a response to the enormous humanitarian needs of the persons and an integral part of UNHCR's three-fold strategy of prevention, preparedness and solutions. We should make every effort to ensure that people are not forced to flee their homes in the first place; but if they are, then we must meet their humanitarian needs and promote conditions which will allow them to return home in safety and dignity. In this way, UNHCR is complementing its efforts to secure asylum abroad with prevention and solution-oriented activities inside the country of origin of refugees and displaced persons.

Prevention and solution, and particularly our work with the internally displaced, are drawing us more directly into situations of internal conflict, and thus bringing us closer to the UN's own efforts to prevent and address threats posed to international peace and security by such situations.

Action by the Security Council to resolve internal conflicts, enforce peace or implement peace settlements can no longer ignore coerced population movements. Security Council resolution 688 found the exodus of 1.7 million Iraqi Kurds in April 1991 to be a major threat to international peace and security. Whether in Namibia or Nicaragua, Cambodia or Mozambique, Rwanda, Liberia or Georgia, Security Council action has consistently recognized the importance of resolving the humanitarian problem as part of the effort to promote reconciliation and reach a political settlement. Indeed, in the case of the former Yugoslavia and Somalia, the Security Council has moved even further, justifying political and military action for humanitarian purposes.

UNHCR welcomes the greater interest of the political arms of the UN in humanitarian problems. For UNHCR, close cooperation with the UN's political initiatives is essential in terms of solving the refugee problem or preventing it from arising. We recognize that humanitarian action can buy time and space for political negotiations. At the same time, however, I am acutely conscious of the risks of politicizing humanitarian mandates. Political and humanitarian objectives are not necessarily coincidental. Repatriation of refugees may be politically desirable but unsafe. Evacuation of civilian populations may meet humanitarian needs but not be politically acceptable.

In analyzing the interface between peacekeeping and humanitarian action, a number of categories can be discerned. I would like to discuss three different categories.

Peacekeeping and Humanitarian Action in Post-Conflict Situations

The first is one in which the peacekeeping and the humanitarian form major components of an overall political framework. The cases of the United Nations Transitional Authority in Cambodia (UNTAC) and the United Nations Operation in Mozambique (ONUMOZ) are good examples.

UNTAC represents a well planned and structured set-up among the different components, including the military and the humanitarian. The key to success was the Paris Peace Agreement, which comprehensively addressed humanitarian and human rights issues in conjunction with the underlying political and military problems. UNHCR, which was mandated to repatriate 370,000 Cambodian refugees, could clearly define its autonomy, neutrality and impartiality under the UNTAC umbrella. It was able to maintain its credibility with and the confidence of all the parties, including the Khmer Rouge in the course of the repatriation, even at times when UNTAC's own relations with the Khmer Rouge were strained.

Mozambique also represents a comprehensive peace implementation scheme by the UN. From UNHCR's point of view, it is a more complex operation than Cambodia, involving repatriation from six countries to Mozambique of about 1.5 million refugees. About 40 percent of them have returned from the neighboring countries to their villages of origin where UNHCR is establishing micro-projects for reintegration. While most of the returns from Malawi are spontaneous, UNHCR is organizing return movements from Swaziland by train, from Zambia and Zimbabwe by bus, from Tanzania by boat and from South Africa through the Kruger National Park! The security conditions created by ONUMOZ will determine the pace of return, as will the ability of UNUMOZ to de-mine the access roads to the returnee areas and to demarcate the mined areas. I hope that ONUMOZ, like UNTAC, will demonstrate the positive interface between peacekeeping and humanitarian action.

Peacekeeping and Humanitarian Operations During Conflict Situations

The second type relates to peacekeeping and humanitarian operations in ongoing conflict situations. UN involvement in the former Yugoslavia is a case in point. UNHCR's operation in the former Yugoslavia predates the deployment of the United Nations Protection Force (UNPROFOR). It started in November 1991, following a request from the then Yugoslav government and the UN Secretary-General to protect and assist persons displaced by the war in Croatia. Following the independence of Croatia, UNHCR was involved in helping not only the internally displaced persons but also refugees who crossed the newly-formed borders. In spring 1992, when the fighting spread to Bosnia and Herzegovina, UNHCR found itself working for the first time in the midst of a raging war and not only for refugees and displaced persons, but also for the besieged population.

UNHCR's close collaboration with UNPROFOR started when Security Council resolution 764 of 13 July 1992 asked UNPROFOR to ensure the security and functioning of Sarajevo airport in order to enable UNHCR to provide assistance to those in need. Furthermore, Security Council resolution 776 of 14 September 1992 authorized the despatch of some 7000 troops to Bosnia and Herzegovina in order to protect and support humanitarian activities. Security Council resolutions 819 of 16 April 1993, 824 of 6 May 1993, and 844 of 18 June 1993 added a further mandate to UNPROFOR to protect "safe areas", areas in which Muslim civilians are under siege by the Bosnian Serb forces.

UNPROFOR also supports humanitarian activities through demining, repair of roads, bridges and utilities, and the running of convoys in some areas. Outside the UNPROFOR structure, UNHCR has benefited from seconded military staff for telecommunications and logistics. UNHCR's airlift to Sarajevo, which now exceeds that to Berlin in 1948, is implemented by air force staff from a number of contributing countries working under UNHCR's authority and control. The airdrop operation is also coordinated with UNHCR and has been a lifeline for many besieged cities.

In these various ways, UNHCR's humanitarian activities have become closely entwined with the military, strengthening our humanitarian capacity but also raising new questions.

Humanitarian access has continued to be based on negotiations with the parties, the military escorts being more of a deterrent than active protection. In the absence of a cease-fire, UNHCR and UNPROFOR have devoted much time and effort to gain assurances for access, very often to have them broken as soon as our convoys began rolling, either because of fighting or deliberate manipulation by the parties. The level of risk has been high, with 11 UNHCR and other humanitarian staff having lost their lives in the past two years.

On the other hand, the possibility of active military intervention has complicated the UN efforts. The non-involvement of UNPROFOR in the combat has allowed the UN to maintain its impartiality and neutrality. If UN peacekeeping forces were to engage in offensive action, it would no longer be possible to maintain the non-political and impartial base of the UNHCR's humanitarian activities, however serious the needs of the victims might be.

In contrast to Bosnia, in Somalia the UN has authorized and used force for humanitarian purposes. The move to justify enforceable action under Chapter VII of the UN Charter was based on the argument that no government existed in Somalia that could request and allow the use of force, and that the situation in that country should be considered a threat to regional peace and security. Thus, Somalia was not a case of intervention against the will of a government but of intervention in the absence of a government.

The Somalia experience highlighted both the difficulties of providing humanitarian action in the midst of total anarchy and the limits of humanitarian action when Chapter VII action is used. The use of force against one party inevitably affects the perceived impartiality and neutrality of the operation. It will take some time to restore the confidence of the Somali people in the UN.

I should mention that UNHCR does not have a large operation in Somalia. We are, however, assisting one million refugees in Kenya, Ethiopia, Djibouti and Yemen. Furthermore, we have since 1992 engaged in a cross-border operation from northern Kenya into Somalia to provide assistance to those who might otherwise feel compelled to leave Somalia.

Integrated Operations

The third type of interface is still somewhat inconclusive. The case in point is Tajikistan, where the integrated efforts of the UN may have helped to prevent the escalation of the crisis, although the situation is still fragile. The civil war in Tajikistan in 1992 displaced over half a million persons and forced another 60,000 to flee to northern Afghanistan. Right from the beginning, UNHCR supported an integrated approach to address the political and humanitarian aspects simultaneously. We participated in the "good offices" mission sent by the Secretary-General in November 1992, and sent in our emergency team in December. It was soon followed by the appointment of the Secretary-General's Special Representative and the deployment of the UN military observers. I believe the joint efforts of all three components helped to create the climate of confidence which in turn encouraged most of the displaced persons and refugees to return home. Today, our main task is to monitor their safety and the human rights situation. All parties in Tajikistan and the neighboring countries have given us their full cooperation in the realization that the humanitarian objective of early return of the refugees and the displaced is crucial for promoting the political objectives of national reconciliation and regional stability. A carefully balanced combination of the humanitarian, political and military components, as in Tajikistan, may well be worth pursuing in some other situations.

Conclusions

Cambodia, Mozambique, Bosnia, Somalia and Tajikistan offer several important lessons.

First, autonomy, impartiality and neutrality are easier to maintain in peacekeeping operations where political objectives of the deployment are clear and accepted by the parties, as in Cambodia, Mozambique or traditional "consensual" peacekeeping. When political objectives are unclear and peacekeeping is launched in the midst of a conflict, as in Somalia or the former Yugoslavia, tensions can and do arise between the political, military and humanitarian components.

Second, whatever the type of operation, it is essential for the humanitarian organizations to maintain the strictly non-political, neutral and impartial nature of their mandates. The provision of humanitarian assistance should not and must not become linked to progress in political negotiations, or to other political objectives. The de-linking must not only be done, it must be perceived to be done.

Third, the neutral and impartial image of humanitarian action can be affected in the context of Chapter VII operations using force, which must by definition be directed against one or more parties. When the UN decides to use military force against a party to the conflict, it may become necessary for humanitarian organizations to distance themselves, if they are to effectively discharge their mandates.

Fourth, the humanitarian mandate must be clearly understood by all. Humanitarian action is not just about providing relief. It is primarily about protecting people and ensuring the basic human rights and security of the victims on all sides of a conflict.

Fifth, closer consultation and coordination are essential between the peacekeeping and humanitarian components at every phase and level. This is particularly so when the two comprise the overall UN effort to achieve peace and security. Coordination is best achieved when the objectives of the particular operation, are set out clearly, the leadership is defined and structures are created to allow open communication among the various components.

Sixth, military resources and expertise are a useful means to accelerate and augment the emergency response capacity of humanitarian organizations. However, military resources for humanitarian purposes should be under civilian command and control.

Seventh, the humanitarian and military actors need to better understand their respective mandates and modes of operation, their concerns and constraints. Thus, UNHCR and other humanitarian organizations have begun a dialogue with the UN Peacekeeping Department to develop operational guidelines and training courses for their staff to improve cooperation and coordination.

Finally, let me say, as inter-ethnic conflicts spread against a background of declining state power, and the media exposes the human suffering, the public pressure for humanitarian action will increase. However, the call for humanitarian action is unlikely to be accompanied by the necessary political will or action to resolve the conflict. The euphoria which greeted the end of the Cold War has been overtaken by a sober reassessment of the new geopolitical realities. In such situations there is a risk that humanitarian action could become a camouflage for political inaction. It could lead to prolonged operations, draining our limited resources, which, unlike peacekeeping, are almost entirely based on voluntary contributions.

The former Yugoslavia has starkly exposed the limits of humanitarian action in the absence of effective political will to address the conflict and the horrendous violations of human rights and humanitarian law. Without peace, humanitarian assistance alone cannot avert disaster. UN peacekeeping and humanitarian activities are of vital importance, but if peace is not forthcoming, they can themselves become hostages of war. There is no substitute for the political will to find a political solution. Such political commitment is essential if peacekeeping and humanitarian action are to remain effective.

Substantive Activities

MILITARY ASPECTS OF UN PEACEKEEPING[1]

by Mats Berdal

The failure of 'coercive disarmement' in Somalia and the continuing involvement of UN forces in the former Yugoslavia have stimulated an ongoing academic and professional military debate about the doctrinal implications of operating in politically fragile and divided communities, in which warring factions only give partial support to the operation, and where there are often no identifiable 'front lines' or legitimate political authorities. Much of this debate has centered on attempts to conceptualise an area of military activity between that of 'classical peacekeeping' and operations based on warfighting doctrines. In a recent comment in *Foreign Affairs*, John Ruggie observed that "the international community must define the new domain of collective military activity that lies between peacekeeping and enforcement."[2] Specifically, a great deal of interest has been generated by attempts to develop a concept of 'second generation multinational operations', in which the key assumption has been that an outside force should not *necessarily* rely on, promote or be

[1] These remarks are adapted from a paper presented by the author to a conference on international peacekeeping held at the Naval War College (US) on 23-24 February 1994. The author would like to thank Charles Dobbie and Roland Dannreuther for their very helpful comments during the preparation of this paper.
[2] Ruggie J.G., "Wandering in the Void: Charterning the UN's New Strategic Role", *Foreign Affairs* November/December 1993.

D. Warner (ed.), New Dimensions of Peacekeeping, 131-136.
© 1995 *Kluwer Academic Publishers. Printed in the Netherlands.*

guided by the need for the consent of the warring factions.[3] According to this view, a peacekeeping force that is properly equipped and underpinned by the appropriate operational concepts and rules of engagement can demonstrate greater 'tactical flexibility' and may engage in various intermediary acts, categories or 'levels' of enforcement.'[4] At the same time, there has been a tendency, most striking in the case of Somalia, to place less emphasis on the requirement of consent as a basis for UN involvement.[5]

To what extent does the actual experience of UN peacekeeping since 1992 confirm the view that the 'international community' must move 'beyond peacekeeping', and, its corollary, that there is a potential area of military activity between 'classic' peacekeeping and large-scale enforcement?

There can be little doubt that the military requirements of UN peacekeeping have dramatically changed in recent years and that this has necessitated a reassessment of operational techniques developed before 1988.[6] Indeed, the experience of large-scale operations between 1991-1994 has exposed the obsolescence of traditional methods of organisation and management, many of which are now clearly undermining the effectiveness of troops and civilians deployed in the field. For example, the lack of a UN contingency planning mechanism and the consequent inability of planners in New York to anticipate logistic requirements largely accounts for the delays in the deployment of troops and civilian staff in Cambodia, the former Yugoslavia and

[3] Mackinlay J., and Chopra J., *A Draft concept of Second Generations Multinational Operations*, Providence RI: The Thomas J. Watson Jr. Institute for International Studies, 1993, pp.4-5.

[4] *Ibid.*

[5] Roberts A., *The Crisis in UN Peacekeeping* Oslo: Institute for Defense Studies, Defence Studies 2/1994, p.16.

[6] For a comprehensive outline of these techniques and methods of operations see *Nordic UN Manual, vols 1 and 2* Jyvaskyla, Finland: Gummerus Kirjapaino Oy, 1992.

Mozambique. An additional and enduring problem is the UN's system of procurement, administered in New York by the Field Administration and Logistics Division (FALD) and by the Chief Administrative Officer (CAO) and his staff in the field. Although the FALD has now formally been incorporated into the Department of Peacekeeping Operations (DPKO), existing procurement regulations continue to complicate and delay the resupply of contingents in the field. The overall responsiveness of units to developments on the ground has consequently been severely reduced. The need for properly trained units, aware of the local conditions and operational requirements, has also been highlighted by recent operations. In addition to this, Somalia and the former Yugoslavia, in particular, have shown that in intrastate, ethnic and communal conflicts, greater attention must be given to force protection, tactical mobility, adequate communications and intelligence support.[7] Above all, they have shown that at the tactical level, a peacekeeping force may have to accept only partial or sporadic consent form warring parties and anticipate casualties. Finally, financial support arrangements for UN field operations remain wholly inadequate.

The UN peacekeeping experience between 1991 and 1994 does *not*, however, indicate that the essence or the defining characteristics of peacekeeping should be abandoned lightly. Peacekeeping, even under the radically changed circumstances of the post-Cold War period, remains a *secondary* activity.[8] As such, it assumes consent at the *strategic and operational* levels, and aims to sustain and promote the level of consent that may exist at the *tactical* level by seeking to act in a manifestly impartial manner. In this it differs sharply from enforcement, in which, *ipso facto*, impartiality and consent have no role to play. The debacle in Somalia in the summer and autumn of 1993 painfully demonstrated the

[7] For a more detailed discussion of these problems see Berdal, M.R., *Whither UN Peacekeeping? Adelphi Paper 281* (London; IISS/Brasseys, October 1993).

[8] James A., *Peacekeeping in International Politics*, London: Macmillan in association with IISS, 1990, p.1.

doctrinally destabilising consequences and political dangers inherent in attempting to merge peacekeeping objectives and enforcement into one operation. UNOSOM II showed that in terms of doctrine there can be no area of military activity between consent-based, impartial operations and enforcement based on war-fighting doctrines.

Through a careful re-examination of the historical record of peacekeeping, and drawing on its own experience in Bosnia, the British Army has arrived at precisely these conclusions by placing consent -- 'interpreted doctrinally at the tactical level as impartiality' -- at the centre of its doctrine for 'wider peacekeeping'.[9] In other words, the range of new tasks subsumed under the term 'peacekeeping' - from electoral assistance and human rights monitoring at one end, to disarmament and demobilisation of irregular forces at the other - still falls within the philosophical framework of traditional peacekeeping:

> "To place them in some fresh category seems not only specious historically but dangerous doctrinally since it would imply that such things as popular support, the conduct of negotiation, mediation and conciliation and the building of confidence and cooperation mattered less post-cold war and that peacekeeping principles might safely be abandoned in favour of a doctrine more oriented towards warfighting."[10]

Although consent will never be absolute, it is the conscious promotion of it, through operational techniques such as minimum force, civil affairs programmes, constant liaison and negotiation, which distinguishes peacekeeping from enforcement. Although in practice, as recent experience has amply demonstrated, contemporary peacekeeping operations "are likely to represent a continual struggle to preserve and sustain whatever consensual framework might exist," the very existence of such a framework means that force may be used without fatally undermining the perception of impartiality that remains essential to

[9] Dobbie C., "Wider Peacekeeping - An Approach to Peacekeeping Post Cold War", (unpublished presentation script), p.5.
[10] *Ibid*: p.3.

preserving the Force's image as a disinterested third party.[11]

It is important to stress that none of this should be seen as in itself ruling out other options or courses of international action to address intrastate conflicts. Proposals, for example, have been made for exploring the idea of UN 'conservatorship' in which the organisation assumes a more comprehensive 'guardianship' role.[12]

In the specific case of the former Yugoslavia, a UN 'trusteeship' for Bosnia was suggested as one way of dealing with the evolving conflict.[13] The central problem throughout the Yugoslav conflict, however, has been the fundamental lack of political will among the Permanent Five for action beyond that of relieving the humanitarian consequences of the war.[14] Given this political reality, maintaining impartiality must remain a critical determinant of operational activity.This essential point has been borne out by the operational experience of UNPROFOR. Reflecting on the "lessons of Yugoslavia," Cedric Thornberry, former Head of Civil Affairs in Zagreb, has noted that "without impartiality, the primary virtue, a UN peacekeeping operation will self-destruct."[15] The difficulty with the 'twin-track' policy of air strikes and the selective lifting of the arms embargo as promoted by the US under President Clinton, was that it would destabilise the operational environment to such a degree that only withdrawal or escalating the level of involvement in favour of one party could be pursued. Given the US administration's consistent refusal

[11] Army field Manual: Wider Peacekeeping (second revised draft) pp. 2-23.

[12] Ratner S.A. and Helman G.B., 'Saving failed States', *Foreign Policy*, Winter 1992-93, No. 89, pp. 3-20.

[13] On the idea of a trusteeship, see Sharp J.M.O., *Bankrupt in the Balkans: British Policy in Bosnia*, London: Institute for Public Policy Research, 1993, pp. 17-19. See also Berdal, M. R. "Fateful Encounter: The United States and UN Peacekeeping", *Survival,* vol. 36, no. 1, Spring 1994.

[14] The current state of the US debate about its future role in UN peacekeeping does not indicate that the US is prepared to contemplate a more long-term and intrusive role in support of future UN efforts to resolve conflict.

[15] Thornberry C., "The Lessons of Yugoslavia", Paper Presented to Centre for Defence Studies seminar, King's College, London, 7 December 1993.

to send ground troops into the area *before* a comprehensive settlement was agreed, withdrawal would have been the only option.[16] As Charles Dobbie notes: "if the impartiality divide is to be crossed, it should be as a deliberate pre-meditated act. It should not be drifted across by accident."[17]

[16] "America welcomes Russian troops for Bosnian mission," *The Times* (London), February 18, 1994, p.17.
[17] Dobbie C., *loc. cit.* (note 8) p.7.

HUMANITARIAN ASPECTS OF PEACEKEEPING

by Sergio Vieira De Mello[1]

In order to address the subject at hand, one should first glance at the definitions of peacemaking, peacekeeping and peace-building in the UN's *Agenda for Peace*. As defined in that document, peacemaking is an action to bring hostile parties to agreement through Chapter VI peaceful means; peacekeeping is the deployment of a UN presence in the field, hitherto with consent of the parties, involving military, police and civilian personnel, both for conflict prevention and the making of peace; and peace-building refers to actions that identify and support structures that strengthen peace and avoid relapses into conflict. All three of these have their own specific humanitarian dimensions.

In examining the relationship between humanitarianism and international security, one sees that there is currently a need to broaden the scope of humanitarianism, which is intimately related to and part of a comprehensive doctrine of the rule of law (i.e. democratization, "good governance" through institution-building, constitutional and legal reforms, information and education, and elections) and human rights. Conflict, as opposed to natural causes, is the most common origin of humanitarian crises. Hence, conflict-resolution must also logically include the search

[1] Former UNHCR Special Envoy for Cambodia and presently Head of Civil Affairs of the United Nations Protection Force in former Yugoslavia (UNPROFOR). The views expressed in this paper are those of the author and do not in any way reflect the official policy of the organisation.

D. Warner (ed.), New Dimensions of Peacekeeping, 137-145.
© 1995 *Kluwer Academic Publishers. Printed in the Netherlands.*

for solutions to humanitarian problems as one of its cardinal elements.

Humanitarian aspects of peacekeeping, therefore, are not one among other dimensions of peacekeeping; they are its very human essence, underpinning and transcending the settlement of military, political and constitutional disputes. For example, only recently was it acknowledged that humanitarian issues ought to figure high on the international security agenda, less for ethical reasons than in response to the element of threat that internal ethnic conflicts, resulting population movements and the disintegration of States represent for the security of other neighbouring or distant countries.

Several lessons about conflict-resolution and the humanitarian dimensions of peacemaking and peace-building can be drawn from the Central American and Cambodian processes.

First, the humanitarian agenda has often created bridges between parties that were either at war or whose diplomatic ties had been severed. In Central America, such a dialogue gradually led to a climate of confidence and mutual recognition that made political negotiations possible. Essential in this process was the mediating role of humanitarian institutions (UNHCR and the ICRC) which acted on the basis of well-established and recognized principles of impartiality, neutrality and humanity, thus depoliticizing highly controversial issues.

Second, during protracted peace negotiations and after a peace agreement, the humanitarian agenda is one on which consensus and cooperative implementation can more easily be achieved. In August 1989, during the first Paris Peace Conference on Cambodia, refugees and reconstruction were the only items on which detailed consensus was reached after nearly two decades of brutal warfare. In the subsequent negotiations leading to a comprehensive agreement in October 1991, and during the implementation thereof, repatriation and resettlement of refugees and displaced persons and the release of prisoners of war were the only areas on which early agreement and operational delivery by *all* the parties -- including the Khmer Rouge -- could be achieved. The principles and operational modalities adopted in 1989 were scrupulously respected by all the Cambodian parties in the 1992-1993 implementation phase, even though other important provisions of the peace agreement were being blatantly violated. All prisoners were set free by early 1992 and by April 1993 all 380,000 refugees had returned freely, without a single serious accident or deliberately disruptive incident, despite the many political overtones of the operation. This helped maintain the momentum of the peacemaking process and contributed to national reconciliation.

HUMANITARIAN ACTIONS AND "PEACEKEEPING" IN HOSTILE ENVIRONMENTS

The call for humanitarian "intervention," as opposed to the extreme notion of "humanitarian war," has been growing. A number of criteria[2] for humanitarian intervention have been suggested, including the following:

- it should be based on the existence or impending likelihood of gross and persistent violations that shock the world's conscience;
- it should be authorized only after all reasonable international and regional diplomatic efforts have failed;
- it must be strictly limited in time and scope, i.e. proportionate;
- it should preserve the territorial integrity of the "receiving" State;
- it should not, to the extent possible, interfere with the authority structure of the "receiving" State, if such a structure exists.

Instances where such criteria may *actually* lead to (military) intervention in a timely fashion are likely to be rare and humanitarian agencies have made it clear that such actions -- however welcome -- cannot *strictu sensu* be called "humanitarian."

[2] By Prof. R.B. Lillich, University of Virginia School of Law.

A great challenge of our time is how to carry out humanitarian actions and "peacekeeping" in hostile environments. I would like to examine three recent examples of this phenomenon: Iraq, Somalia, and the one I am more familiar with, the former Yugoslavia.

In Iraq, Security Council Resolution 688 established a direct link between refugee flows and cross-border incursions on the one hand, and a threat to international peace and security on the other. Some believe that the latter justification prevailed over the former. I do not see that as a flaw *per se*. What is unfortunate, however, is the apparent use of the argument of a threat to international peace and security to *prevent* cross-border movements so as to impose an in-country solution. Doubt about the wisdom of this lingers, unresolved, in my mind even today. Secondly, it is a fact that Security Council Resolution 688 was largely made possible (although narrowly adopted by only nine positive votes) by what Adam Roberts calls the logic of the rights of victors over a defeated country. It may be right to say, as a result, that this was a *sui generis* episode.

In Somalia, the logic of intervention (by UNITAF first and by UNOSOM later) was inspired less by humanitarian concerns than by the need to substitute for the lack of governmental authority and to tackle the resulting anarchy which endangered peace and security in "the entire region." What was so often presented as a "humanitarian mission" eventually turned out to be a political disaster as a result of the conflicting roles of two estranged actors - the US and the UN - in the Mogadishu area, even though the operation scored many unacknowledged successes in other parts of Somalia. After overengaging military forces, the United Nations and some troop-contributing nations were forced to partially disengage themselves in a clear admission of incompatibility among imposed disarmament, enforcement of peace and reconciliation, the creation of a new, unitary government and the pursuit of humanitarian goals under the same mandate and flag and with essentially the same actors.

In former Yugoslavia, the mandates of UNPROFOR and UNHCR are tightly interwoven, yet must retain their specificities. I shall examine UNPROFOR's unenviable role before I review, under a separate and final heading, the new set of challenges humanitarian agencies face in conflict situations. Let us consider UNPROFOR's humanitarian aspects, understood in the broader meaning suggested at the outset.

In the former Yugoslav Republic of Macedonia (FYROM), UNPROFOR has deployed a military contingent and established a small civil affairs presence in the context of preventive diplomacy: that is, with a view, *inter alia*, to forestalling an outbreak of internal fighting between different communities, external interference, mass human rights violations and population displacements. Institution-building should also become a priority task in FYROM. This is precisely what the international community (the UN, the EU, the CSCE and individual interested States) were unable to achieve in other republics of the former Yugoslavia. Foreseeing and neutralizing trends leading to manmade disasters is also, logically and chronologically, an essential humanitarian dimension of that sort of preventive "peacekeeping."

In Croatia, UNPROFOR's original mandate, based on the Vance Plan, was essentially to establish its presence in territories occupied by Serb forces (UNPAs), disarm the latter, protect the civilian populations -- including, of course, minorities -- and ensure the return of refugees, through or as part of a political settlement. Beyond its clear political purpose, such a mandate was and remains primarily humanitarian, and herein lies the contradiction. Although UNPROFOR has achieved remarkable humanitarian results through its military, police and civilian components (e.g. prevention of further widespread brutalities against minorities; monitoring of local police and courts; promotion of family visits and reunions; organization of local Red Cross meetings and, through them, distribution of family parcels and messages; assistance to the delivery of humanitarian aid; formulation and implementation of small, mainly agricultural economic projects) the primary political objective -- which, in turn, could bring about an effective solution to the problems of refugees, displaced and missing persons, prisoners, and other humanitarian questions -- remains as elusive as ever. Despite the diplomatic and military energy and resources deployed first by the European Union -- including the fielding of its first Monitoring Mission, ECMM -- and later by the UN at all levels -- including UNPROFOR initiatives in the field -- the impasse over Krajina remains a glaring reminder that a relapse into conflict is an ever-present likelihood. The truth of the matter is that the humanitarian role of a peacekeeping force such as UNPROFOR in Croatia is a mere and frustrating palliative in the absence of a political settlement.

In Bosnia-Herzegovina, UNPROFOR was the first "peacekeeping" force to be given an exclusively humanitarian mandate in the context of an all-out and merciless war. Greater contradiction in terms and, indeed, on the ground, would have been difficult to achieve. Since June 1992, UNPROFOR was successively mandated to: take over and protect Sarajevo's airport and ensure the safe flow of UNHCR humanitarian aid; protect the safe transit of UNHCR land convoys and the delivery of their assistance; protect six "safe areas" and their civilian populations - even though no delineation of their boundaries and no formal requirement for their demilitarization existed!; and reopen and control Tuzla airport for humanitarian purposes. In addition, it was mandated to control heavy weapons within an exclusion zone (EZ) of 20 kilometers around Sarajevo and, later, Gorazde, and supervise their withdrawal from that zone, as well as to interposition itself along the confrontation lines in those areas to ensure respect of the cease-fire. Subsequently, the Security Council called for total freedom of movement into, out of, and within Sarajevo as well as for the rehabilitation of essential public services in larger Sarajevo and the restoration of normality for its population. Moreover, as a result of the cease-fire agreement signed on 23 February 1994 between the Bosnian Government and Croat forces and of subsequent political progress achieved in Vienna and Washington between the parties, UNPROFOR now is not only required to separate forces and supervise the withdrawal of weapons all along the confrontation line in Central Bosnia, but also to demilitarize Mostar.

This list of incremental tasks, most of which are clearly humanitarian, is impressive and often paradoxical, and unfairly exceeds UNPROFOR's resources and capacity to deliver on the basis of traditional peacekeeping operational procedures and rules of engagement in an openly hostile environment. The following provisional lessons can be drawn from this situation. First, despite systematic harassment and interference, warfare, direct attacks, sabotage, adverse terrain and weather conditions, and the frustration and despair of its personnel, UNPROFOR and UNHCR have, by and large, managed for nearly two years to reduce the proportions of the disaster and to ensure the survival of millions of victims in Sarajevo and throughout Bosnia-Herzegovina. Second, through its own assertiveness -- admittedly insufficient -- or external support (e.g. NATO's imposed exclusion zones and the threat of use of air power at UNPROFOR's request), UNPROFOR was able -- admittedly belatedly -- to prevent mass human rights violations and further population exoduses, such as in Vares in November 1993, and to turn tragedies into achievements, as in the case of the Sarajevo Market massacre and the subsequent relative restoration of normality. Thirdly, it is clear that, as in Croatia, unless a comprehensive political settlement is achieved, no significant, lasting and effective progress can be made towards the resolution of the overwhelming humanitarian problems of Bosnia-Herzegovina. These include the return or resettlement of refugees and internally displaced persons; the release of prisoners and information about the fate of the missing; and peace, dignity and rehabilitation for the population at large. In other words, humanitarianism is not and should never serve as a substitute for diplomatic action, especially when responsibility for the former is shared with a peacekeeping force.

Clearly, a change of perspective is called for. How can a humanitarian mandate be preserved in an unsuccessful "peacekeeping operation?" The above cursory review clearly illustrates the expanding trend towards integrating the political, military and humanitarian, *latu sensu,* objectives in conflict-resolution. This integration is welcome, yet uneasy. If humanitarianism is to be understood as covering a spectrum broader than the mechanical distribution of humanitarian aid, and if it encompasses the protection of human rights and the prevention and possible reversal of population movements, then it is essential that intergovernmental and non-governmental humanitarian agencies retain a degree of independence from political and, particularly, military activities.

It is, in fact, also in the interest of the political and military sectors that the specificity of the humanitarian mission be recognized and preserved, not least by the parties to the conflict. When all other types of dialogue are broken, the humanitarian channel must remain open, as it did between UNHCR and the Khmer Rouge in Cambodia. Not only can it provide access to victims, but also better understanding of the respective positions of the parties and a basis for the eventual restoration of confidence and resumption of negotiations.

Access, assistance and protection to all those in need requires that humanitarian agencies act in a spirit of total neutrality and impartiality and that their actions under no circumstances be politicized by any of the actors in a given conflict. The contradiction between the essentially political act of sanctions and its humanitarian consequences is a telling non-military example of the predicaments faced by humanitarian agencies. The problem of suspension of aid and withdrawal of staff in situations of extreme danger or blatant disregard of principles and commitments is one that humanitarian agencies should address jointly and separately from political considerations. Integration need not mean confusion, subordination or merger.

CONCLUSION

In conclusion, there is clearly little doubt that the humanitarian aspects of peacekeeping operations occupy an ever-increasing space in the latter's mandates. They are overwhelming, as we saw, in the case of UNPROFOR in Bosnia-Herzegovina. Severe critics of such integrated approaches, such as MSF in the case of Somalia, as well as those who fail to uphold the specificity and independence of humanitarian action in conflict situations, are both in the wrong. It must be realized that in a fast-evolving world where conflict -- particularly domestic -- obeys new patterns, it is only natural that the peacekeeping and humanitarian doctrines and practices should undergo a difficult period of transition leading to a mutually-reinforcing co-existence. The political, the military and the humanitarian are not dissociable, as we often said, to no avail, in the 1970s and 1980s. The key to a successful synthesis lies less in the equation of humanitarianism and peacekeeping than in the ability to politically resolve conflicts of the latest generation before both humanitarian action and peacekeeping are discredited.

STATE BUILDING AND DEMOCRACY IN SECOND-GENERATION PEACEKEEPING OPERATIONS

by Ronald Dreyer[1]

State building and democracy have been on the agenda of United Nations activities since the inception of the organization. In 1948, the United Nations observed by-elections in Korea and since then, monitoring elections has been a regular feature of United Nations activities in the context of decolonization, particularly through the monitoring of plebiscites and referendums in Trust and Non-Self-Governing Territories in Africa and Asia during the 1950s and 1960s.

The UN involvement in the decolonization process culminated in the successful transfer of power in Namibia in 1990, after the inhabitants of "Africa's last colony" had elected a Constituent Assembly for an independent Namibia during the same week in November 1989 in which the Berlin Wall crumbled. For the first time in the United Nations' history, armed contingents of peacekeepers and unarmed military and police observers as well as electoral observers operated within a single United Nations peacekeeping operation.

[1] The opinions expressed in this paper are those of the author and do not necessarily reflect the views of the United Nations.

D. Warner (ed.), New Dimensions of Peacekeeping, 147-155.
© 1995 *Kluwer Academic Publishers. Printed in the Netherlands.*

After the Cold War: State Building and Democracy Through UN Peacekeeping Operations

After the end of the Cold War and the collapse of socialism as an ideological alternative to Western liberalism, democracy and political pluralism became a tenet of a new post-Cold War "world order". The end of the Cold War also signalled a new role for the Organization of the United Nations in the era of state building and democracy, in particular in the domain of supervising and at times organizing elections. With the end of the Cold War, the United Nations Secretariat was vested with a new legitimacy for solving various regional and civil wars in which the belligerents previously had their respective allies and protectors in both the United States and the Soviet Union. Peace agreements between the former enemies were reached in Cambodia, El Salvador, Angola and Mozambique. In some countries such as El Salvador and Cambodia, the United Nations played an active peacemaking role during negotiations, thereby helping to bring about the successful conclusions of peace agreements. In all the abovementioned countries, the implementation of the peace agreements was, and in the case of Mozambique presently is, monitored by the United Nations.

Elements of state building and democracy play an important role in the implementation of the agreements. Known as peace building, they have their conceptual bedding in the Secretary-General's *Agenda for Peace* of 1992, which proposes a framework for a comprehensive approach to peacekeeping operations. Preventive diplomacy, political peacemaking, peacekeeping and at times peace enforcement are now linked to *peace building* measures. The aim of peace building is to strengthen the peace process once hostilities have ended. Contrary to classical peacekeeping operations whereby United Nations troops keep the warring parties apart pending a political settlement, the United Nations now also engages in emergency humanitarian assistance. Moreover, it attempts to contribute to state building and democracy, for example through supervising or organizing elections. Such elections are most often seen as the culminating point of the peace process. However, elections do not always prevent the outbreak of renewed fighting, as the cases of Angola and Cambodia have shown.

The supervision of an electoral process (voter registration, political campaign, polling and counting of ballots) by United Nations observers is an important peace building activity, preceded and accompanied as it is by the supervision of military confidence-building measures, namely the holding of a cease-fire, assembly and disarming of troops as well as their demobilization and the formation of a new unified national army and police force. The integration of troops and police in a national army and police force would create, together with the holding of credible presidential, parliamentary and sometimes municipal elections, the necessary conditions for state building and democracy in the process of post-war reconstruction.

The degree of United Nations involvement in state building and democracy as part of second-generation peacekeeping operations varies. Whereas the United Nations was responsible for organizing the elections in Cambodia, it merely observed the electoral process in Angola. In El Salvador, the monitoring of the electoral process was linked with an active UN role in the investigation of human rights abuses, the creation of a national ombudsman of human rights and the establishment and training of a new police force.

Assessing the Success of the UN's Role in State Building and Democracy as Part of Second-Generation Peacekeeping Operations

After the holding of free and fair elections in Angola, which had been monitored by the United Nations, the war between the Angolan government and the UNITA opposition movement redoubled in intensity compared to the Cold War period. In Cambodia, the active involvement of the United Nations in state building and democracy could not prevent renewed fighting between the new Cambodian government and the Khmer Rouge. In El Salvador and in Mozambique, it is too early to make a statement as to the effectiveness of the UN in the peace process at the time of writing (June 1994). In El Salvador, the presidential race was completed as late as April 1994 and in Mozambique, elections are scheduled to take place in October 1994.

What are then the possible obstacles which can prevent the United Nations peacekeeping operations from contributing more successfully to state building and democracy in countries which emerge from a civil war? Several factors may help to explain why peace accords can be difficult to implement in spite of a sometimes large presence of United Nations peacekeepers.

Most importantly, the *lack of a common political will* to fully implement a peace agreement and to respect the results of elections whatever their outcome, will obviously prevent the successful implementation of a peace agreement, culminating as it should in the holding of transparent and credible multi-party elections. This common political will of the former enemies to bring a peace process to its successful conclusion did exist in El Salvador, where both the government and the opposition FMLN were willing to make sometimes painful compromises in favor of the peace process such as the disarming of the former guerrillas and the Salvadoran government's acceptance of United Nations investigations into human rights violations. In Angola, on the other hand, the common political will for seeing the peace process through did not exist, marred as it was by profound mutual distrust between the Angolan government and UNITA. In an inversion of the famous saying of Clausewitz, politics was seen as the continuation of war rather than war being the continuation of politics. In the absence of a common political will to see a peace process through, United Nations human rights, political and electoral observers, however qualified and numerous they may be, cannot contribute in any significant manner to post-conflict state building and democracy.

This absence of common political will is borne out and sometimes reinforced by six related elements: the former enemies' pledge to compete against each other in elections; mistrust between the former belligerents; the absence of a transitional government; an incomplete unified territorial administration; basic human rights which are not guaranteed; and a United Nations mandate which ends shortly after the holding of elections without ensuring the monitoring of post-electoral state building.

Peace agreements between former belligerents contain one inherent contradiction which can be dangerous if not addressed adequately. The former enemies notably pledge themselves in peace agreements, such as the peace agreement between the Angolan government and UNITA of May 1991 and the Rome Accords between the Mozambican government and RENAMO of October 1992, to contest conflictual democracy through elections. But how prepared are the former enemies to "fight" elections in a spirit of reconciliation towards their former adversary who now has become merely a political rival? As the tragic events in Angola have shown, confidence-building measures such as disarming and demobilization of troops as well as the formation of a unified national army verified by the United Nations were not sufficient to overcome the contradiction between the mentalities of war and peace. The loser of the September 1992 elections (UNITA) refused to accept the election results and decided to return to war with an army which had not been sufficiently demobilized nor disarmed during the phase preceding the elections. In the words of one Angolan observer, the elections had been free and transparent but without peace.

Related to the above, profound mistrust between the former enemies often continues to prevail among influential sectors of the signatories of a peace accord, such as the armed forces. This mistrust is often very difficult to overcome in the relatively short transition period allowed for between the signing of a peace agreement and the holding of elections.

Moreover, peace agreements do not set up transitional governments whereby the former enemies would be able to demystify enemy images of the past through day-to-day collaboration. The setting up of consultative joint commissions as in the case of Angola and Mozambique do not allow for a pragmatic joint governing which is indispensable for reducing mutual distrust. If the concept of coalition government is discussed, it is not determined before the elections, contrary to what was the case in the constitutional talks in South Africa. Rather, the possibility of a coalition government is most often conditional on the outcome of elections. However plausible this might be in a society with no recent history of civil war, the possibility that the former enemy could hold state power on his own to the exclusion of its main political rival is likely to perpetuate the "enemy image" compounded by the continued mistrust between the two former belligerents.

In the field of state building, the establishment of a unified territorial administration is indispensable for guaranteeing the conditions for free and credible post-conflict elections. As a result of civil war, separate territorial administrations in the areas controlled by the respective former enemies continue to co-exist within one national territory. This can enhance distrust between the signatories of the peace agreement and prevent the formation of a state above party politics as guarantor of peace and basic human rights. But in countries such as Cambodia and Angola, war factions (Khmer Rouge and UNITA) continued to exert military and *de facto* administrative control over parts of the national territory, thus preventing the establishment of a unified national administration with freedom of movement for parties and individuals as a prerequisite for the holding of free and fair elections. But often, the mandate of the United Nations peacekeeping operations is not strong enough to put effective pressure to bear on the signatories in favor of unified territorial administration. At times, such as in Mozambique, the unification of territorial administration is even outside the mandate of the United Nations.

The adequate monitoring of human rights is often lacking in second-generation peacekeeping operations. If the right to life is generally guaranteed through the holding of a cease-fire, the respect of basic human rights such as freedom of movement, association and expression is not a foregone conclusion. However, these basic political rights are indispensable ingredients for creating the conditions conducive to fair and above all credible elections. The establishment of a neutral and unified police force which can guarantee the respect of these basic political rights is therefore indispensable. But the police components of United Nations peacekeeping operations are often too weak to guarantee the establishment of a neutral police force and, moreover, the human rights component within a second-generation peacekeeping operation is most often weak or non-existent.

One notable exception is the United Nations operation in El Salvador (ONUSAL) where the existing government police force was reorganized and trained with the assistance of United Nations police observers. Furthermore, and in this El Salvador was innovative, ONUSAL helped to create an ombudsman for human rights. This no doubt contributed significantly to creating conditions for the presidential, parliamentary and municipal elections which were held in El Salvador in March 1994 (with a run-off second round for the election of a new president). In Angola, on the contrary, state building, which is indispensable for successful elections, was very fragmented. Incomplete disarming of government troops and UNITA, partial demobilization, the existence of a national army only on paper, the non-unification of the national administration and no serious attempts to create a national police did not create the necessary conditions for respecting the outcome of the results of the September 1992 elections which were technically free and fair.

Lastly, it is very difficult to successfully complete state building in post-war societies within the short life span of a peace process ranging from the conclusion of a cease-fire to the holding of elections. Likewise, United Nations officials involved in peace building activities are most often obliged to leave the country shortly after the holding of elections. "Peace building monitors" such as police and human rights and political observers are thus prevented from monitoring the progress of state building and democratic institutions beyond elections in the larger context of national reconstruction.

TOWARDS ENHANCING THE ROLE OF THE UNITED NATIONS IN STATE BUILDING AND DEMOCRACY

In view of the potential factors which can impede the successful implementation of a peace process and hamper the satisfactory fulfilment of the United Nations mandate, several conditions, if met, can enhance the effectiveness of United Nations peace building activities within a peacekeeping operation.

1. In order to guarantee the common political will between the former belligerents during the implementation of the peace agreement, the United Nations, through its representatives in the field, should be officially recognized and accepted as an active mediator between the signatories of the peace agreement and all other parties involved during the entire peace process.
2. The United Nations should always combine political peacemaking through an active role in the negotiations of a peace agreement with an active involvement in the implementation of the agreement. This has been the case in El Salvador, where the United Nations has been able to contribute to the successful implementation of the agreement. Early and active participation of the United Nations in the negotiation of a peace agreement should be a precondition for accepting a substantive involvement in peacekeeping and peace building.
3. The peace agreements should contain provisions which allow for the establishment of a transitional government between the former enemies. Only through day-to-day governing can the deeply ingrained distrust between former belligerents be reduced and the common political will to see the peace process through be enhanced.
4. The holding of multi-party elections can be meaningless without the creation of an environment which is conducive to free, fair and credible elections. While traditional peacekeeping activities such as assembly, disarming and demobilization of troops continue to play a vital role in this endeavour, the active involvement of the United Nations in the monitoring and verification of basic human rights should always be an

important part of a peacekeeping operation which includes a contribution to state building and the holding of elections.

5. In order to enhance the process of state building and democracy after the holding of elections, human rights and political observers should continue to monitor the process of political reconstruction. If they are given the mandate of mediating between the different political groups in the country, they may be able to contribute to preventing an often fragile peace from breaking down and military conflict from erupting again.

MANAGING PEACEKEEPING

MANAGING PEACEKEEPING FROM A LEGAL PERSPECTIVE

by Ralph Zacklin

As defined by the United Nations in its *Agenda for Peace*, peacekeeping is a United Nations presence in the field -- normally including military and civilian personnel -- with the consent of the parties concerned, to implement or monitor the implementation of arrangements relating to the control of conflicts and their resolution and/or to protect the delivery of humanitarian relief.

Peacekeeping is considered to be one of a range of means employed by the United Nations for the maintenance of international peace and security; the others are preventive diplomacy, peacemaking, peace-enforcement, and peace-building.

In recent years, the distinctions between these various means have tended to become blurred in the political and public eye. For example, three case studies examined at this Colloquium represent very different types of operations and yet all of them are placed under the rubric of peacekeeping.

Insistence on clarifying the nature and meaning of peacekeeping is not merely a lawyer's obsession with clarity and legal definition; it is necessary because the legal character and nature of the operation has a direct bearing on the legal issues which arise and their resolution. The more the different means become interrelated, the greater the need for clarity.

The role of the legal adviser in managing peacekeeping is multi-faceted. It involves:

D. Warner (ed.), New Dimensions of Peacekeeping, 159-162.
© 1995 *Kluwer Academic Publishers. Printed in the Netherlands.*

- providing legal advice and assistance directly to the Secretary-General, and participating in the Secretary-General's Task Force on United Nations Operations;
- giving legal advice on request to the President of the Security Council and to the Council as a whole, especially in informal consultations;
- drafting and negotiating agreements and other types of legal arrangements (e.g. SOFAs) and following up with advice on the interpretation and implementation of such agreements/arrangements;
- providing legal advice on administrative, financial and personnel matters, including contracts.

Advice given by the UN Legal Counsel covers constitutional law questions, public international law, internal administrative law and private law.

The successful management of peacekeeping presupposes a number of preconditions: a clearly defined and attainable mandate; full political and financial support of member states; consent and cooperation of all the parties; and clear lines of command.

Let me elaborate on these preconditions, beginning with the question of the mandate. For legal purposes, the management of peacekeeping begins with the adoption by the Security Council of the relevant resolution. This basic document should set out clearly what the mandate is, in political and legal terms. The political goals should be consistent with the legal powers of the Security Council and should be legally attainable. Lack of clarity will give rise to legal and political difficulties which can undermine the operation, as was the case with Security Council resolution 837 which created UNOSOM II.

On the second point, support of member states, it is clear that full political and financial support of member states is absolutely essential to the success of a peacekeeping operation.

Much of the debate on financing these operations has focused on searching for measures to remedy the abysmal situation of the Organizations's financing.

Peacekeeping assessments are legally binding obligations of Member States under Article 17 of the Charter of the United Nations, and a failure to pay incurs a breach of the Charter. Legal redress is, however, limited to Article 19 which is not a very useful tool. There is a real need for mechanisms that counter indebtedness and provide effective sanctions for illegality.

In addition to financing, support of peacekeeping operations includes the provision of personnel and equipment. Legal arrangements such as troop-contributing agreements and letters of assist have been developed to secure such personnel and equipment.

Novel questions have arisen regarding the status, safety and security of personnel in such operations, as well as what laws are applicable to, for example, air crews, seconded personnel, and internationally contracted personnel.

Thirdly, the consent and cooperation of all the parties concerned is a *sine qua non* of peacekeeping. In terms of legal arrangements, this is translated into the SOFA which is concluded with host countries. It has become increasingly difficult to conclude satisfactory SOFAs. One reason for this is the difficulty of entering into and maintaining respect for legal arrangements with non-UN-recognized entities such as non-recognized governments and movements. This is a problem for peacekeeping because the conclusion of a SOFA is a precondition for approval of a peacekeeping operation.

Finally, the command structure must be clear, and must function properly. The principle of UN command is that peacekeeping operations are international in character and are carrying out a mandate entrusted to them by the Security Council. The forces are an integrated unit that falls under the authority of Security Council and under the command of the United Nations, i.e. the Secretary-General, which means they take no orders from external sources.

In the cases where peacekeeping operations have experienced difficulties, these problems have been the result of a failure to observe the principle of United Nations command, as with UNOSOM in Somalia, or of inadequate coordination between headquarters and the field or at headquarters and in the field, as with UNPROFOR in the former Yugoslavia.

THE CONFUSION BETWEEN PEACEMAKING AND PEACEKEEPING

by Maurice Bertrand

An attempt to identify the various types of action by the United Nations in the field of peace and security has been made in the report published in July 1992 by the UN Secretary-General, entitled *An Agenda for Peace*.

The definitions of the concept of peacemaking and peacekeeping given in Chapter II of this document are the following:

- *peacemaking* is action to bring hostile parties to agreement, essentially through such peaceful means as those foreseen in Chapter VI of the Charter of the United Nations.
- *peacekeeping* is the deployment of a United Nations presence in the field, hitherto with the consent of all parties concerned, normally involving United Nations military and/or police personnel and frequently civilians as well.

The other concepts proposed to classify the possible actions of the United Nations in this chapter of the *Agenda* are *preventive diplomacy* ("action to prevent disputes from arising between parties, to prevent existing disputes from escalating into conflicts and to limit the spread of the latter when they occur") and *post conflict peace building* ("action to identify and support structures which will tend to strengthen and solidify peace in order to avoid a relapse into conflict.")

Another notion is proposed in Chapter IV of the *Agenda for Peace*, i.e. *peace enforcement*, which means "restoring and maintaining

D. Warner (ed.), New Dimensions of Peacekeeping, 163-171.
© 1995 *Kluwer Academic Publishers. Printed in the Netherlands.*

cease-fire by force," (the "peace enforcement units," more heavily armed than peacekeeping forces, placed under the command of the Secretary-General "should not be confused with the forces that may eventually be constituted under Article 42 to deal with acts of aggression.")

These definitions seem clear. In fact, the successive chapters of the *Agenda* show that, even theoretically, the distinction between these different forms of actions is blurred, and that there is confusion among them, particularly between peacemaking and peacekeeping and between preventive and corrective action. The practice followed by the Security Council has, equally, shown that permanent confusion existed.

I will try, first, to demonstrate the existence of this confusion, and second, to explain the reasons for it and draw some conclusions from this situation.

The Conceptual Confusion

The conceptual confusion between *peacemaking* and *peacekeeping* in the *Agenda for Peace* seems to be due to the following reasons. First, the conception of peacemaking itself is not clear and not very convincing. It is very difficult to find a distinction between *peacemaking* and *preventive diplomacy*. Both refer to preventive action, either before or during existing conflicts, and to chapter VI of the Charter. It is very difficult to understand why the two notions have been singled out as different types of action. Both concepts imply the use of diplomatic skills only. This kind of intervention does not seem to have been efficient in the past when used on actors who had already decided to enter into a war. No indication is given of the methods through which the traditional impotence of these attempts could be overcome.

Paragraph 34 of the *Agenda* says:

> "If conflicts have gone unresolved, it is not because techniques for peaceful settlement were unknown or inadequate. The fault lies first in the lack of political

will of parties to seek a solution to their differences through such means as are suggested in chapter VI of the Charter, and second to the lack of leverage at the disposal of a third party if this is the procedure chosen."

This quotation shows:

- first, that the authors of the *Agenda* still believe in the possible efficiency of interventions on actors like those enumerated in chapter VI of the Charter, i.e. a total illusion....
- second, that, despite the mention of the notion of "leverage" there is no indication of the type of leverage that would be needed. The only one in this chapter concerns sanctions and use of military force, and amelioration through assistance to displaced persons, with the regret that resources are not available. There is also, in paragraph 40 of the *Agenda*, a reference to the "collective efforts of the United Nations system" that could "improve its contribution to the peaceful resolution of disputes" by reinforcing coordination in the Administrative Committee on Coordination (i.e. wishful thinking about the capacity of the agencies to help in this regard and about the possibility of better coordination).

Despite the fact that paragraph 15 of the *Agenda* says that the aims of the UN must be "to address the deepest causes of conflict: economic despair, social injustice and political oppression," there is absolutely no indication of the possibility of acting on the situations which lead to conflict, for example through economic assistance. The reason for this fundamental lacuna could be that the Security Council has no economic leverage at its disposal. But in these conditions, it is difficult to understand why in the chapter on post conflict peace building the utilisation of economic and social assistance for building peace is so precisely envisaged. For example, paragraph 56 says: "in the aftermath of international war, post conflict peace building may take the form of concrete cooperative projects which link two or more countries in a mutually beneficial undertaking that can not only contribute to economic and social development but also enhance the confidence that is so fundamental to peace," and paragraph 57 says "only sustained cooperative work to deal with underlying economic, social, cultural and humanitarian problems can place an achieved peace on a durable foundation." It remains to be explained why it seems possible to use economic assistance after the end of a conflict and not before, in order to avoid the conflict itself.

The conception of *peacekeeping* in the *Agenda* is even less clear than that of peacemaking. Its first definition is perfectly correct. Paragraph 50 of the *Agenda* enumerates the basic conditions for success and says that they "remain unchanged": i.e. "a clear and practicable mandate; the cooperation of the parties in implementing that mandate; the continuing support of the Security Council; the readiness of member states to contribute the military police and civilian personnel, including specialists required; effective United Nations command at Headquarters and in the field; and adequate financial and logistic support."

But if this conception, including in particular the "cooperation of the parties in implementing the mandate," has been applied, it can be said without exaggeration that, with the exception of Namibia and El Salvador (and perhaps Cambodia), none of the so-called "second-generation peacekeeping operations" undertaken after 1988 would have been started. By insisting in paragraphs 50 to 54 on the "new array of demands and problems" that "has emerged regarding logistics, equipment, personnel and financing," the *Agenda* shows that the new type of operations is directed more at peace building than at a strict peace keeping, and that, in fact, the operations would have to take place even if the "settlements negotiated by peacemakers" have not obtained the full and serious cooperation of the parties. It is this ambiguity that makes it difficult to find exactly where to situate the dividing line between peacekeeping and peacemaking. This is even clearly acknowledged in paragraph 45 of the *Agenda*, which states that "there may not be a dividing line between peacemaking and peacekeeping. Peacemaking is often a prelude to peacekeeping, just as the deployment of a United Nations presence in the field may expand possibilities for the prevention of conflict, *facilitate the work of peacemaking* and in any case serve as a prerequisite for peace building."

This is a candid acknowledgement that the philosophy which has inspired the majority of the new operations has been that the display of military force (either traditional peacekeeping units or forces close to the notion of peace enforcement) was the main instrument for establishing and stabilizing peace in situations where the acceptance of the conditions for peace by the various parties was in fact non-existent. This military approach toward peacemaking, which the *Agenda for Peace* has helped to develop, has proven to be a mistake.

The practice of the Security Council has shown that this philosophy has also been adopted by its members and that this confusion has led to failures.

Practical Confusion

It would be very difficult to find numerous examples of peacemaking by the UN during its first four decades. Every Secretary-General has attempted to play a role and to make available his "good offices," but the cases in which they have been used are very rare and their successes even rarer. This is not the place to recount the history of the UN, but it seems important to note that, in general and for the main problems, diplomatic activities aiming at the establishment of peace have been monopolized by politicians and diplomats of the great powers. To give only some examples, peacemaking in the conflict between Israel and the Arab states has been, at least since the 1960s, the domain of the US Secretaries of State or even of the Presidents (Rogers in 1970, Kissinger in 1974, Jimmy Carter in 1979, Baker in the 1980s, etc.), the role of the UN being limited to establishing the various peacekeeping forces around Israel. The more recent examples of this tendency to reserve peacemaking for the great powers and to call upon the UN only after a settlement has been reached are Cambodia (for which the Paris agreements were negotiated by four powers), Namibia (where the American negotiator obtained the departure of the Cuban troops and the cease-fire), Nicaragua, etc.

The most important role of the UN in peacemaking until the end of the 1980s was to carry out the preparatory work. It should be recalled that in the Iran-Iraq war, the good offices of Secretary-General Perez de Cuellar and the Olof Palme mission began very early, and that Security Council resolution 548 of 20th July 1987, which was immediately accepted by Iraq, was finally used by Iran when it decided in 1988 to put an end to the war. In the same way, the negotiation of the Geneva agreements concerning Afghanistan lasted eight years, but Mikhail Gorbachev found them very useful when he decided to withdraw Soviet troops from the country. Finally, for Namibia, it was the Secretary-General's plan, ready years in advance, that was used to facilitate the accession to independence of this country, when the US-led negotiations succeeded. The UN work in all these cases offered some pretext for adopting a solution. It is not a useless role, but it is not the most glorious or the most important one.

However, the role attributed to the UN has become different since 1990. It is an absolutely new one, since this type of utilisation of the organisation was occasionally practiced before, but it has become generalized.

The practice consists of referring to the UN problems which are considered insoluble or at least very difficult. Examples of this practice can be found in the case of the UK giving up its mandate on Palestine in 1947, in the case of Congo in 1960, and in Cyprus, at least since 1974. Since 1990, this kind of quasi-insoluble problem has developed in Western Sahara, Angola, Yugoslavia, Haiti, Somalia, Mozambique, etc. The UN interventions requested by the great powers are still called peacekeeping operations. But to be kept, peace should already exist, and in all the cases mentioned, this was and still is not the case.

The first practical confusion is due to the title given to these operations. In fact, they are not peacekeeping ones. They should be called "peacemaking undertakings through the use of the blue helmets."

This could be easily shown by considering the interventions. I will limit my examples to Somalia and Yugoslavia, without entering into a detailed analysis.

In Somalia, the intervention was belated: the civil war was already going on in 1986-1987 and it developed into a full war in 1988-1990, followed by the secession of Somaliland in 1991. The Security Council was requested to react only in 1992.

Moreover, the first resolution, 733 of 23rd January 1992, decided on an arms embargo which was too late to be effective, but was obviously intended to facilitate peacemaking. The other resolutions of 1992 on humanitarian activities, the sending of observers, the creation of UNOSOM, and the various actions undertaken in the following years cannot in any way be called peacekeeping operations, but rather clumsy attempts at peacemaking through the display of blue helmets, peace enforcement through American intervention, and humanitarian relief accompanied by numerous unsuccessful appeals to the parties to stop fighting.

For Yugoslavia, a similar analysis can be made. Peace has not existed there since 1990. All of the efforts made, here again far too late, and without any use of economic assistance, have, since the first resolution (713 of 25 September 1991), attempted "to restore peace and dialogue" through the sending of observers, the use of numerous blue helmets and the convening of various conferences and meetings. They have been accompanied by humanitarian operations. But the display of the blue helmets has not in any case been able to keep peace; no cease-fire has been respected. Again, it would be better to qualify the UN intervention since its origin as "a clumsy peacemaking operation using humanitarian activities, military display, and diplomatic negotiations."

CONCLUSION

The existing confusion between peacekeeping and peacemaking leads to questions more far-reaching than the simple problem of definition. It is the very conception of these UN interventions that needs to be questioned, in the following ways:

1) Are the policies followed by the UN Security Council based on a thorough analysis of the underlying causes of intrastate conflicts? Has the UN an explanation for the multiplication of these conflicts?
2) Is it possible to establish peace in intrastate conflicts by using a military display, plus diplomatic negotiations, plus humanitarian activities?
3) Would it be possible to try to influence the situations which lead to conflicts rather than trying to influence, without any leverage, the actors in the conflicts?
4) What kind of leverage could be used in this regard? Is it possible to mobilise enough economic and financial resources to modify the situations which lead to conflicts?
5) How would it be possible to use these resources before conflicts arise?
6) Is the present structure of the UN and are the powers of the Security Council sufficient to permit more efficient peacemaking interventions?

These questions are very difficult to answer. It seems obvious that the methodology which is now applied to these situations of conflict is not the right one; that there is room for a thorough reflection on the causes of these intrastate conflicts; that it is time to give serious consideration to the necessity of developing preventive action (not only so-called preventive diplomacy); that, to give only one example, the question of doing something to stop the development of a civil war in Algeria should be carefully studied now and an answer given to it as soon as possible.

But at the same time it is necessary to acknowledge:

- that this does not seem to be the main concern of the governments and of the public of the great powers;
- that it is easier to obtain resources for humanitarian relief or for military interventions after conflicts have arisen than for economic interventions of the "Marshall Plan" type to avoid conflicts;
- and, finally, that the UN is not equipped to deal with the use of economic resources, these types of interventions being in the domain of the International Monetary Fund, which is not in charge of security problems. A structural reform of the UN system would be necessary to correct this situation, and such a reform is not under consideration.

But the apparent impossibility of correctly solving these problems seems to me to render it indispensable to give thorough consideration to them.

THE FORMER YUGOSLAVIA: NATO'S ROLE

by Elie Marcuse

Whatever the theoretical definitions, peacekeeping in practice encompasses a number of instruments or tools for maintaining or encouraging peace. In this broad sense, NATO has a range of tools for peace. As an example, I will briefly describe NATO's response to the situation in Bosnia-Hercegovina.

The NATO actions in February and the beginning of March are likely to be significant turning points in the conflict in the former Yugoslavia. The February 9 ultimatum and the February 28 enforcement action for the UN resolution -- shooting down Serbian planes -- did not come as bolts out of the blue.

NATO's active involvement in the former Yugoslavia began with *monitoring,* in July 1992, of the UN's trade embargoes and, in October 1992, of the UN's ban on military flights. Later, in April 1993, NATO moved to the *enforcement* of these UN decisions. From the time NATO's operation Deny Flight began until March 1994, over 11,000 sorties were flown. This operation effectively denied the use of air power by all three factions as an important instrument of war. The only case of a significant military violation was the incident which resulted in the downing of four of six Serbian planes on February 28.

As for the enforcement of the embargoes, more than 2,500 vessels were boarded or diverted. It is impossible, of course, to estimate how many vessels were deterred from attempting to breach the embargoes, but since enforcement began, there were no violations up until March.

D. Warner (ed.), New Dimensions of Peacekeeping, 173-179.
© 1995 *Kluwer Academic Publishers. Printed in the Netherlands.*

Eleven were detected beforehand.

In July, 1993, NATO moved to provide UNPROFOR with protective air cover if called upon. That is, should UNPROFOR units come under attack in the performance of their mandate, they could call upon fighter aircraft to defend them. The next month, the Alliance approved an option for air strikes, with the authorisation of the United Nations Secretary-General, if the strangulation of Sarajevo and other safe areas continued. NATO coordinated closely with the UN Secretary-General and UNPROFOR to work out the planning. As a result, the Serbs began to withdraw from the commanding heights of Mount Igman in the weeks immediately after the early August warning.

The NATO Summit in January renewed this air-strike option and reiterated the urgent humanitarian need to lift the siege of Sarajevo. Against this background, the mortar attacks against civilian targets in Sarajevo in the first week of February were fateful. They prompted the UN Secretary-General to ask NATO to prepare for the use of air strikes to prevent further attacks. The North Atlantic Council issued the decisive warning on February 9 to create an exclusion zone around Sarajevo. Virtually all heavy weaponry was withdrawn or placed under UN control by the expiration of the deadline 10 days later. NATO also welcomed the role played by diplomacy, including by Russia, in helping to secure this outcome. Diplomacy, however, can rarely succeed if not backed by credible actions. When necessary, enforcement is crucial in order to preserve the effectiveness of deterrence and to preserve the credibility of UN resolutions. After NATO's action of February 28, there can be little doubt about NATO's credibility or resolve.

NATO's role in peacekeeping, however, is broader than the dramatic events of February 1994. What I would like to do in the remainder of my discussion is to describe how NATO went from its Cold War role to today's missions, in which peacekeeping plays an ever-increasing part. I will first set out, in more detail, the policy background; then, describe what NATO has to offer as tools of peace; and, thirdly, indicate the way ahead, following January's NATO Summit which made several decisions of significance for NATO's contribution to peacekeeping.

THE POLICY BACKGROUND

NATO's move towards a peacekeeping role was not an overnight affair. The first step was the new Strategic Concept, or strategy, for NATO agreed by the 1991 NATO Summit in Rome.

Building on the Alliance's highly developed and integrated multinational capability, the new Strategic Concept set out several elements significant for NATO's future involvement in peacekeeping:

- First, the strategy included a new appreciation of the risks of instability in Europe. Alliance leaders agreed that NATO must be capable of responding to such risks;
- Second, the Strategic Concept set out a new approach to crisis management. Reflecting the more complex and diverse nature of the new risks, the Allies agreed to restructure their forces to increase their flexibility, mobility, and multinationality.

In short, then, the new Strategic Concept laid the basis for NATO's role in peacekeeping. The failure of the international community to deal adequately with the developing crisis in the former Yugoslavia led to the next step in the evolution in Alliance policy and to NATO's explicit acceptance of a peacekeeping role.

In June 1992, NATO Foreign Ministers, at their meeting in Oslo, deplored the deterioration of the situation in the former Yugoslavia. They also agreed to make Alliance resources and expertise available for peacekeeping. This decision established the basis for NATO's involvement in peacekeeping. Let me therefore explain this decision in greater detail:

- First, the offer was made to the CSCE, and later the UN, to enhance the means of these two bodies in managing NATO's available assets. It was an offer to *support, not to undertake*, peacekeeping activities;

- Second, the Alliance itself would decide on a case-by-case basis when and how to participate in peacekeeping activities; and
- Finally, NATO's participation in a peacekeeping operation would *not* preclude the participation of other parties. NATO's Military Authorities were asked specifically to consider how non-NATO countries could be involved in NATO's peace support operations.

Not only did the NATO decisions in Oslo establish an explicit peacekeeping role for the organization, they also entailed a military role for NATO beyond its treaty area. This also arose in the context of the debate on peacekeeping in the UN that culminated in the UN's *Agenda for Peace*. Boutros-Ghali's report devoted a whole chapter to cooperation with regional arrangements and organisations. One passage is particularly worth quoting because of its relevance to NATO: "... regional arrangements or agencies . . . possess a potential that would be utilised (for) preventive diplomacy, peacekeeping, and post conflict peace building."

WHAT NATO HAS TO CONTRIBUTE

I see two kinds of contributions that NATO could make. First, NATO unites the efforts of North America and Europe, including, significantly, both the US and the EU; this means that among NATO's members are many of the most active contributors to UN peacekeeping operations and three permanent members of the Security Council, as well as, frequently, one of the rotating UNSC members. NATO also has the strength of close links with countries in the east of Europe and beyond. The North Atlantic Cooperation Council's Ad Hoc Group on Peacekeeping brings together all 16 Allies, our 22 Partners, and other countries such as Finland, Austria, and Sweden who play a significant role in UN and CSCE peacekeeping efforts. In the year since this group was founded, it has developed a better common understanding of peacekeeping, both conceptually and practically.

The second contribution is NATO's military assets. They are a unique array of tools to support and strengthen diplomatic efforts: a standing military framework under well-tried mechanisms of political control; forces that are capable, credible and trained to operate in a multinational context; and a military planning capacity which maintains close links with national planners. This allows the timely preparations of multinational military assessments and plans based on extensive national information resources.

Increasingly, there is a need for military forces that are *capable*, as opposed to *symbolic*; that can respond rapidly if required, and that are prepared and exercised in a multinational context, in contrast to the often isolated, national deployments of the past.

THE WAY AHEAD

Let me turn to the future. NATO seems destined to undertake missions other (Art. 4) than collective defence of its members (Art. 5). These missions are and will remain essential for the North Atlantic Alliance. That means that we have to be even better prepared than we are now. The NATO Summit in January charted the course.

Most prominently, the Summit launched *Partnership for Peace*. The Partnership is primarily designed to forge new security relationships with the East. This initiative, however, has important peacekeeping aspects. Special emphasis will be placed on creating an ability to operate with NATO forces in such fields as peacekeeping, search and rescue, and humanitarian operations. To promote close military cooperation and interoperability, NATO is proposing peacekeeping field exercises beginning this year.

Secondly, summit leaders endorsed the concept of Combined Joint

Task Forces as a means of facilitating contingency operations. The peacekeeping significance of CJTFs lies in the creation of new mobile capabilities. The Alliance's command structure, though extensive, is static and was designed primarily for collective defence against a major threat. The CJTF will provide the Alliance, for the first time, with deployable and mobile commands. Instead of having hastily to construct an untried HQ, as happened in Bosnia with UNPROFOR (which drew on assets from NATO's Northern Army Group HQ), the CJTF units would be established, trained and ready to respond.

The CJTF concept will lead to greater flexibility in other ways, as well. It will provide capabilities that can be used, by common agreement and on a case-by-case basis, either by NATO or the WEU, thus enhancing the capability of the Europeans to respond to crises. It will also facilitate the participation of non-NATO countries in operations with Allied countries. In short, the NATO Summit considerably expanded the possibilities for peacekeeping cooperation and took a major step in putting the assets and facilities developed within the Alliance to a wider use for the benefit of peace and stability in the whole of Europe.

Conclusion

Let me now conclude by emphasizing four points.

- First, as for the problems at hand, the Alliance is making a significant contribution to operations in the former Yugoslavia by making available its unique assets and expertise to the United Nations.
- Second, for the longer term, the Alliance has been working to promote a broader international capability to respond to peacekeeping requests through cooperation with its partners to the East;
- Third, the Summit in January gave a major impetus to NATO's role in peacekeeping by initiating Partnership for Peace and CJTF, which further expand the possibilities for peacekeeping cooperation;

- Finally, in expanding its tools for peace, the Alliance is building on the lessons of international experience in Bosnia. Deterrence remains a valid instrument of peace; enforcement capability is crucial to credibility; and diplomacy remains paramount in finding solutions.

SUMMARY OF COLLOQUIUM ON NEW DIMENSIONS OF PEACEKEEPING

by Connie Peck

The Colloquium sought to review, analyze and critically examine the development of peacekeeping as it has evolved in response to the new set of complex conflict situations which have confronted the UN in recent years. It was acknowledged that peacekeeping is only one of a number of means available to the UN in its effort to maintain international peace and security. This summary seeks to highlight the major themes and issues which were discussed and to summarize the various proposals for improving future practice.

THE EVOLUTION OF PEACEKEEPING

1. First-Generation Peacekeeping Operations (PKOs)

The "first generation" of peacekeeping was created in response to the Suez Crisis, whose special conditions shaped the early model. Lester Pearson used the British and French argument of intervening on behalf of the international community as a *de facto* international police force to establish a UN force to replace the British and French (UNEF). One principle that was enunciated in the establishment of this first peacekeeping operation was that in order to isolate crises from the Cold War, the Permanent Members of the Security Council would not take part in such operations.

D. Warner (ed.), New Dimensions of Peacekeeping, 181-204.
© 1995 *Kluwer Academic Publishers. Printed in the Netherlands.*

In response to subsequent crises, further peacekeeping operations were established by mandates from the Security Council or the General Assembly to fulfil an international task. A consensus of both the parties and the superpowers was needed before such operations could take place. Peacekeeping was intended as an emergency measure which would buy time to settle the dispute. The goal of early peacekeeping was, therefore, to stop or freeze the conflict rather than to settle it (i.e. "conflict management" rather than "conflict resolution"). Three legal principles were used as a basis for action: a) autonomy of the operation; b) autonomy of the state, which would be respected by the operation, and c) non-use of force except in self-defense.

Over time, however, several problems presented themselves: 1) actions of PKOs sometimes had an effect on the balance of power within a country, thus making it difficult to separate the international and internal aspects of a situation; 2) in situations where one party gave consent but then reneged, it became difficult to know what to do (e.g. Katanga in the Congo); 3) in some situations (e.g. Cyprus), peacekeeping became a substitute for resolving the dispute.

2. Second-Generation PKOs

In the mid-1980s, with the relaxation of tensions in the Cold War, a new type of PKO emerged which involved the implementation of a prior peace agreement (e.g. in Namibia, Cambodia, and El Salvador). Since most of the situations to which this new type of peacekeeping was applied were internal, the civilian components of these operations were increased. These new PKOs included tasks such as the repatriation of refugees, election monitoring, implementation of human rights agreements, civil administration, and various other post-conflict peacebuilding tasks.

3. Third-Generation PKOs

The end of the Cold War and the subsequent vacuum created by superpower inaction created a number of complex conflicts and humanitarian crises. As a result, between 1991 and 1994, peacekeeping operations grew dramatically in number and size as the UN tried to respond to these problems. At the end of 1993, there were 70,000 peacekeepers in the field, and the peacekeeping bill for that year was three times the regular budget of the UN.

This rapid expansion without a sufficient infrastructure, as well as the extraordinarily difficult nature of the situations themselves, led to new kinds of actions by the Security Council, as well as by peacekeepers in the field, and brought to the fore a number of new problems.

Current Problems and Challenges

1. The Nature of Current Conflict Situations

While ethnic, religious and internal conflicts are not new, the UN's involvement in such situations is relatively new and a number of participants pointed to the need to better understand the complex problems that such conflict situations pose, including the difficulties of dealing with non-governmental parties. Moreover, the problems of failed or collapsed states also present the difficulty of operating in a fragile political environment with no legitimate political authorities. One speaker predicted that this phenomenon of intrastate conflict is just the beginning and that the process of change will accelerate, requiring an urgent and a deeper analysis of all aspects of the problem.

2. The Erosion of Standard PKO Doctrine

It was noted that the era of First-Generation PKOs was gone forever since the international community was now facing completely different types of challenges and could no longer tie itself to the original principles. Principles such as non-participation of the Permanent Members of the Council or neighboring countries in peacekeeping operations have been eroded by recent practice. Good judgment was needed to replace doctrinal precepts, since general rules could no longer be applied to particular crises.

Related to this, several participants highlighted the sheer complexity and difficulty of issues that the decision-makers at all levels (on the Security Council, at UN Headquarters and in the field) are facing. Decisions based on thousands of facts have to be taken quickly, sometimes within the hour. Agonizing choices have to be made between different principles and different requirements. Inevitably, some mistakes are made. By studying the outcomes and consequences of these decisions, however, future decision-making can be improved.

It was noted that if judgment was the most important rule, this raises the question of the composition of the Security Council and whether it sufficiently represents the concerns of the Member States as a whole.

3. The Need for Clearer Mandates and "Status of Force Agreements"

Clarity of the mandate given by the Security Council to peacekeeping operations is essential since it not only states what an operation can do, but also provides a legal basis for these actions. Lack of clarity can undermine an operation. Resolution 688 (regarding the Kurdish situation in Iraq), for example, was extremely unclear about whether it came under Chapter VI or VII, and led to a dispute between the Permanent Members of the Council and the Secretary-General on the one hand and the Legal Office on the other. Another illustration was Resolution 837, which was adopted in the aftermath of the attack on peacekeepers in Somalia and which authorized all necessary measures to be taken against those responsible, including their arrest, prosecution and punishment. The resolution, however, was taken without due consideration as to how it would be implemented. The Security Council took the decision over a weekend, in haste, and apparently did not consider the legal issues, such as under what law accused perpetuators could be tried, by what court, and so on, causing grave problems for the entire operation. Routine consultations between the President of the Security Council, or the Security Council as a whole, and the Office of Legal Affairs should facilitate clarity and improve coordination.

Further, it was noted that the conclusion of a "Status of Force Agreement" should also be a precondition of approval of peacekeeping operations by the Security Council. One of the major problems in Yugoslavia was that troops were deployed in a very large-scale operation without a Status of Force Agreement and, hence, without an agreement with any of the parties.

4. The Need for Better Coordination

Coordination of multiple actors carrying out multiple types of interventions with varied mandates represents another problem. In some situations, the UN, regional organizations and bilateral actors act in contradictory ways. Early action by multiple actors in the former Yugoslavia is a case in point. The recent coordination between the UN and NATO is an exception and an example of the complementary advantage which could be achieved from better coordination.

The need for better coordination between Headquarters and the field was also emphasized, as well as the need for a closer relationship between Member States and the Secretariat. It was suggested that a better consultation process is needed to keep Member States, especially troop contributors, involved and committed to PKOs.

5. Mixing Peace Enforcement and Peacekeeping

This was perhaps the most discussed issue. The recent practice of the Security Council in giving mixed mandates to PKOs (i.e. including mandates which invoke Chapter VII) has caused confusion about the difference between peacekeeping and peace enforcement, which is full of hazards for peacekeeping practice (as demonstrated by UNOSOM II in Somalia). Peacekeeping assumes consent at the strategic, operational and tactical levels, and without such consent, peacekeeping could self-destruct.

Several participants warned that peace enforcement is an entirely different kind of instrument than peacekeeping, and that mixing peace enforcement with peacekeeping involves a number of inherent dangers which have to be fully understood and appreciated before such a decision is taken. Understanding the differences between the two types of instruments is vital for making a decision to "cross the Rubicon" as one participant termed such a decision. Once this line is crossed, there can be no return to peacekeeping.

Several participants also stressed the danger of the "slippery slope," i.e. allowing a peacekeeping operation to slip into a peace enforcement operation without due consideration to the consequences. The importance of making this decision in a deliberate and premeditated way rather than drifting across this boundary was repeatedly stressed. It was emphasized that there is not a spectrum, but a crucial point beyond which the operation changes.

Loss of impartiality with its attendant consequences was discussed extensively (e.g. as occurred in UNOSOM II). In such situations, the UN comes to be perceived as a party to the conflict, which leads to a choice between escalation and withdrawal. One participant suggested that in some instances, the UN may eventually decide to abandon its impartiality doctrine and "throw its lot in with the legitimate government."

All participants agreed that maintaining impartiality in the humanitarian field is essential, although the difficulties of delinking humanitarian and political/military actions can be significant, as is discussed further below.

Other consequences of mixing enforcement and peacekeeping were discussed and include:

- Peace enforcement involves different logistics, rules of engagement and command structures, which makes such a change difficult at best.
- Humanitarian operations can be greatly endangered by such a change.
- Consent of parties for future peacekeeping operations may be less forthcoming if the Security Council can change an operation from peacekeeping to peace enforcement.
- Such a practice could present problems for troop contributing countries, especially neutral countries.
- Troop contributing countries would have to think twice before offering troops, since the decision to involve one's country in a war involves a totally different political analysis and decision-making process. This could further slow deployment of peacekeeping forces.
- Once the operation becomes one of peace enforcement, impartiality cannot be restored.
- Peace enforcement by one PKO will have adverse consequences on others.
- Peace enforcement is difficult for the public to understand.

One participant suggested that if an operation such as UNOSOM II is to be used in the future, it should not be called "third-generation" peacekeeping, but, rather, that it would be better to consider deployment of distinct peace enforcement units as mentioned in *An Agenda for Peace*.

A hybrid of peacekeeping practice, that has been termed "robust peacekeeping," was discussed at some length. It involves a more assertive practice of peacekeeping, as advocated by General Rose in Bosnia. This form of peacekeeping could include measures such as rapid air strikes used in self-defense if the source of fire against peacekeepers was known. It was argued that, if it were carried out immediately as a self-defense measure, no party would challenge its use. "Robust peacekeeping" would also mean that troops would exercise their right to freedom of movement (as was done in Gorazde) without negotiating an agreement each time with the parties. Instead of asking for permission to deliver humanitarian aid into a conflict zone, troops would simply exercise this right.

Another participant warned that from the perspective of the parties, air strikes may not be seen as self-defense, and he pointed out that, in any case, an enforcement action taken in self-defense does not solve the larger problem.

It was also mentioned that the use of force does not necessarily have to imply Chapter VII, and that in some cases force may be used within a consensual framework in an impartial manner.

6. Chapter VII and Peace Enforcement

The legal representative from the UN Secretariat noted that the use of Chapter VII does not imply that force will necessarily by used, but merely that a resolution is enforceable.

Several participants suggested that "law without force means nothing," but others questioned whether imposing a solution or coercing parties to agree to one will lead to long-term solutions and compliance.

There was general agreement that when and if force is used, it needs to be used skillfully. Most participants agreed that threats should not be made unless they are backed by resolve and political will. It was argued that, in many cases, the skillful threat of force would enable the international community to avoid using it. Other participants, however, warned about the hazards of brinkmanship and the consequences of the failure of such actions. One participant noted that there may currently be undue optimism about this option in the aftermath of the successful use of the NATO ultimatum.

The use of force in an intrastate conflict such as Somalia was raised and the following questions asked: Are precision air strikes and ground actions going beyond the strict re-establishment of law and order, and, rather, trying to change the political landscape? Should the UN be acting as though it were involved in warfare or in a police operation? Are air strikes in downtown Mogadishu consistent with the efforts to establish a good government? Is retaliation in response to an attack on its peacekeepers something the UN wants to promote? The participant observed that intrastate conflicts were not being distinguished from interstate conflicts and advocated a more "people-centric approach," since the will of the people forms the basis for the authority of governments.

Several people mentioned that the UN simply lacks appropriate command and control structures to launch a full-scale peace enforcement action. As a result, the UN will have to continue to rely on Member States for command, intelligence and control structures in enforcement operations.

The participant from NATO stressed the advantages of NATO in this regard, pointing to its unique array of military assets, its close links with national planners, including three of the Permanent Members of the Security Council, its joint planning and military exercises with some of the most active peacekeeping Member States, its new security relationship with the East through the "Partnership for Peace" program, and its new push toward deployable and mobile commands which can respond quickly to problems.

He noted the complementary role that NATO had played in the former Yugoslavia through monitoring the trade embargo (by boarding or diverting 2,500 vessels), through its denial of air power to all three factions (by flying 11,000 sorties), and, finally, through the success of its recent ultimatum.

Sanctions were also mentioned briefly. It was noted that sanctions only work when applied against democratic countries where the population can put pressure on the government, otherwise they penalize the population and legitimize the government (as exemplified in the former Yugoslavia).

7. Protection of UN Personnel

Some of the problems faced by peacekeeping operations relate to the protection of peacekeeping troops. Along with the increase in the size and complexity of operations, the threat to UN personnel has also increased dramatically. The impact of such losses on the willingness of countries to contribute troops was noted; some felt that Member States may need to be brought to the realization that in some cases "peace comes at a price."

Two initiatives for providing better protection of UN peacekeepers -- each with a somewhat different approach -- have been raised in the General Assembly. One approach (sponsored by Ukraine) is to develop a new international legal instrument. A second approach (advocated by New Zealand) suggests that UN peacekeepers should become internationally protected persons and that harming them should make the perpetrator liable for prosecution in a criminal proceeding.

A difference of opinion also exists within the Secretariat about this issue. Some argue that the problem is becoming so grave that it requires a strong response; others argue that the UN has to deal with the very people who are attacking their personnel and that criminalizing them makes this impossible.

One participant noted that instituting the protection of humanitarian workers puts humanitarian issues in a new light, as the "initiators of military action," similar to the way the killing of missionaries in colonial times brought about military operations.

One unresolved issue is how such laws would be applied in situations where the UN was involved in an enforcement action. Privileging UN forces by giving them superior rights to protection or the use of force might pose serious hazards by departing from the laws of war.

One short-term remedial measure might be the hiring of expert staff to assist the security coordinator. The Secretariat should be asked to inform the Security Council whether or not the security arrangements for its personnel are adequate.

8. "Political Will" and The Use of Positive Incentives or "Carrots"

Insufficient "political will" was often cited as a source of problems. This includes both the political will of third parties to become involved in a conflict, and that of the parties themselves to resolve their conflict. Both were mentioned as major stumbling blocks in the context of the former Yugoslavia.

One participant observed that the UN was overstretched, like a colonial power, leading the Security Council to act "selectively" based on factors such as "perceived self interest," the "CNN effect" and other variables, rather than on the basis of principle or the dictates of the Charter. Hence, conflict situations such as Afghanistan (since the Soviet withdrawal), Angola (since the failed elections), Sudan, Rwanda, and others go unattended while vast resources are poured into other situations. Problems for the legitimacy of the organization (involving the issue of the composition of the Security Council), as well as the crisis of democracies in responding only to the latest Gallup polls or upcoming elections were both mentioned in this context. Factors such as fatigue also affect the response -- in the case of Burundi, the crisis came at the wrong time, when the international community was exhausted from its efforts in Somalia and Yugoslavia.

"Political will" also affects decisions about what type of action the UN will take in a situation, and was widely felt to be lacking in the international response to events in the former Yugoslavia. It was noted that if missions become more risky, through an increased use of peace enforcement measures, this could further erode political will. One participant mentioned that there is a need to develop a stronger imperative for collective action to uphold international norms and values, and to redefine self-interest as collective interest.

Several people mentioned the need for at least a minimum of "political will" among the parties. There was discussion of the need for "carrots" as well as "sticks" as one means of increasing political will. One participant asked what carrots the UN had at its disposal. The Special

Representative of the Secretary-General for Cambodia responded by noting that in Cambodia, the assistance with postwar rehabilitation was one of the primary "carrots" available to the international community. All four Cambodian factions were deeply moved by the pledges of assistance from the international community which exceeded the appeal of the Secretary-General. He proposed that other "carrots", such as recognition, appreciation or participation could be used more effectively by the UN.

9. Management, Logistic and Procurement Problems

The lack of a relationship between the decision-making process of the Security Council and the availability of resources continues to be a major source of problems for the UN (as illustrated in the tragedy resulting from the late deployment of peacekeepers in Namibia which was due to ACABQ and the Fifth Committee being too slow to approve the budget). The organization continues to operate in an *ad hoc* and *a posteriori* manner which is unworkable with fifteen PKOs in the field. In Cambodia, for example, only three of the seven components were ready when the Paris Accord was signed, and the costs of the delay were severe -- contributing to the claim of the Khmer Rouge that the UN had not been able to create a neutral political environment and, therefore, the Khmer Rouge's contention that it need not fulfil its obligations.

Arrearages on peacekeeping contributions also greatly constrain the work of the organization. Resources are so tight that various peacekeeping operations have to compete with one another for resources and attention from Headquarters. The current legal redress under Article 19, that those in arrears will lose their vote in the General Assembly, does not work.

It was mentioned that bureaucratic rules imposed by the General Assembly in the name of efficiency often work against substantive efficiency and cause problems for operations. One of these is the UN system of procurement, which requires multiple bidding for every item and which continues to complicate and delay troops on the ground.

The UN Departments at Headquarters are so underresourced that they are unable to anticipate logistical needs or to carry out satisfactory contingency planning. Integrated task forces (such as were available in the Namibia operation) are needed to facilitate communication and decision-making between Headquarters and the field, but are impossible in the current situation, where 15 field operations are being managed by a small staff at Headquarters.

Coordination in the field is inadequate, as well. Lack of coordination between the political and military components in UNOSOM Headquarters in Mogadishu resulted in the civilian side having no warning of what the military side was going to do; hence proper legal advice could not be provided. Coordination was also a major problem in Cambodia.

The chain of command for peacekeeping operations runs from the Security Council to the Secretary-General. The current Secretary-General believes that the responsibility must always rest with the Political Heads of the organization and the Military Commanders should report to the Civilian Commanders. This is why Force Commanders are always appointed at the ASG level.

Lack of respect for command structures can also cause problems. There should be no orders from external sources, as occurred in several instances where national troops are said to have taken orders from national sources, causing enormous difficulties. Integrated units would help to overcome this difficulty.

It was suggested that the Secretariat should, when necessary, make it clear to the Security Council that a given mandate is difficult or impossible to execute (as occurred when the Secretariat circulated a non-paper on the "Safe Havens" Concept, arguing that 34,000 troops would be needed to carry out the operation).

Finally, there continues to be a lack of properly trained military and civilian units.

10. The Interface Between Humanitarian and Peacekeeping Operations

Since the end of the Cold War, there has been a growing awareness that humanitarian issues cannot be treated in isolation from other security issues. Resolution 688 (regarding the Kurdish problem in Iraq) was the first instance of a humanitarian situation being identified as presenting a major threat to international peace and security. Since then, humanitarian operations have become the *raison d'etre* for several peacekeeping operations. In Somalia, the mandate to put an end to grave and massive violations was a clear breakthrough in international humanitarian law. Other issues, such as coerced population movements, can no longer be ignored and will need to be better addressed by the Security Council in the future.

Dealing with the sources of humanitarian problems is, of course, the real challenge for the international community. Humanitarian issues can also play a positive role in getting the peacemaking process started, as they did in both Central America and Cambodia. Agreement on humanitarian action is sometimes easier to achieve, and can buy time and space and create a better political environment (as occurred in the first Paris Peace Conference, which was otherwise considered a failure, but where principles about the repatriation of refugees were agreed on by all four parties and gave momentum to the peace process).

Discussion centered on the dangers of politicizing humanitarian mandates and the complex relationship between humanitarian goals and political and military operations. The problems can range from humanitarian objectives becoming a camouflage for inaction (as in the former Yugoslavia) to their becoming a pretext for enforcement, thus causing additional humanitarian problems (as occurred in Somalia). The use of humanitarian assistance as a palliative in a situation where there is not sufficient political will to bring about a peace agreement (on the part of either the parties or the international community) was sharply criticized. Several speakers highlighted that lack of effective action imposes grave injustice on the population as well as on humanitarian workers, and they also noted the corrosive effect it has on international norms and law which ultimately undermines and discredits the international organisation involved. It was noted that Yugoslavia has exposed the limits of humanitarian action in the absence of political will, and that if peace is not forthcoming, humanitarian action could become the hostage of war.

At an operational level, while military components can actually assist humanitarian goals in some cases (e.g. when they are able to keep open an airport so that humanitarian goods can be delivered, when they de-mine or when military drivers are willing to drive convoys in situations where civilians refuse), there are other situations where association between military and humanitarian operations jeopardizes humanitarian objectives and actually places such operations and its workers in great danger.

The importance of humanitarian operations remaining impartial was stressed, as well as the need to (in some instances) delink them from the military and political components of an operation. The difficulty in achieving this delinking in the perception of the parties, however, was also discussed, especially in cases where enforcement is used.

Sanctions also complicate humanitarian operations, since certain goods must be exempted. The relationships between the various components work best when the political objectives are clear and accepted by the parties, when the mandate of protecting people and ensuring the safety of victims is clear, and when there are good structures for carrying out the operations. In addition, military support for humanitarian operations needs to remain under civilian command and control. UNHCR is currently working on a set of operational guidelines for humanitarian operations which may assist in overcoming some of these difficulties.

To improve humanitarian assistance, it is also necessary to improve the capacity of the agencies. Although UNHCR now has an emergency capacity, there is still a gap between its emergency capacity and its ability to tackle a new problem on a long-term basis. The most difficult problem is to find enough qualified people.

The relationship between UNHCR and the ICRC is a close one and illustrates the complementarity that can exist between international organizations and NGOs when they work together.

More recently, in certain circumstances, UNHCR has become involved with assisting internally displaced persons. The UN needs to further consider its assistance to internally displaced persons, since no agency currently has a mandate to assist them and since the problem is enormous, and growing.

11. Democracy and State Building

Since Namibia, PKOs have been increasingly associated with democracy, which has led to an underlying tendency to assume that multi-party democracy will lead to peace -- which isn't always the case. Indeed, it was proposed that there may be a qualitative difference between societies involved in and free of conflict and that the very nature of a post-conflict society makes the realization of Western-style democracies a distant goal.

It was noted that peacekeeping operations cannot, in themselves, create democracy or state building -- instead, they can create an environment that enables local actors to achieve their goals. Peacekeeping operations can sow the seeds of democracy, but it is the people in the country themselves who need to nurture these seeds. To accomplish this goal, peacekeepers need to work closely with the population and local institutions to help them understand what a participatory democracy involves, including the meaning of human rights. The UN's role in helping to achieve this also needs to be clearly specified.

Being involved in state building, however, requires cultural sensitivity. Those heading such operations need to be careful not to adopt a position of intellectual arrogance in imposing their own values or decisions in a country with a strong tradition. Involvement of the parties in making their own decisions, and assistance in helping them to resolve differences, provides them with experience in the process of democracy and a model for peaceful conflict resolution. The Special Representative of the Secretary-General for Cambodia noted that although some criticized his insistence on conciliation, the four months he spent working with the Cambodian parties to arrive at a joint decision on electoral laws was well worth the effort in terms of demonstrating the process of democratic decision-making. When we see Cambodia under a unified government with two leaders who previously swore that they would be mortal enemies until they died, the UN can be said to have done a good job.

Moreover, universal standards such as those on human rights cannot be imposed but have to be accepted, since compliance has to come from the people themselves. Establishing mechanisms to provide an ongoing promotion of these norms is one way to foster them. Cambodia may now have more human rights NGOs than any other country. Peacekeeping operations have to develop and be integrated with local institutions in order to have a lasting effect.

The UN's roles as the administrator of peace agreements, as mediator of disputes regarding peace accords, and as a guarantor of the successful implementation of peace accords are sometimes difficult to reconcile and balance, particularly in situations of decaying consent (such as in Cambodia).

One participant noted that a culture of participatory democracy with prior experience of elections or other participatory processes increases the probability of success in such operations. He hypothesized that this may, in part, explain why Angola -- where there had never been an election -- was unsuccessful, whereas El Salvador, where there is a tradition of democracy, appears to have a better chance of success.

Measures to gradually restore trust between the parties are also an important part of the process of post-conflict peacebuilding. One speaker stated that confidence building and mediation are the daily bread of those involved in state building actions, but the latter can be tricky since it involves suggesting measures without appearing to interfere. Codes of conduct for political parties, civil education of former soldiers and the population as a whole, training in human rights for police and others, confidence-building measures, and in some cases, transitional governments of national reconciliation can all facilitate this process.

The peace agreement itself is important to the success of such missions and can determine how far a peacekeeping operation can progress toward democracy and state building. Accords which include structural changes, such as changes to institutions, human rights monitoring or land reform are more likely to bring about long-term solutions to age-old grievances.

Another participant stressed this point by suggesting that peacekeeping operations should be called PCBOs - Peace Consolidation and Confidence-Building Operations. The goal of these kinds of operations is to integrate the fighters of one party into the civil society of the other and to consolidate the emerging peace with the help of third parties.

Peacekeeping operations are, however, only the beginning of the rehabilitation process. They prepare the political conditions for socio-economic reconstruction. Equal attention should be given to the social and economic rehabilitation of post-conflict societies.

12. The Japanese Role in Peacekeeping

Japan's new role in peacekeeping stems from criticism by its allies of its non-military role in the Gulf War, in spite of the fact that it contributed 13 billion dollars to this effort, which had to be financed by a special tax. The passage of a new law by the Diet in June 1992 enabled Japan to contribute military personnel to UNPKOs in a logistics capacity when a ceasefire is in place, when the parties have given their consent, and when peacekeepers are acting in an impartial manner. In response, Japan has sent troops to a number of PKOs. Although there was fear that neighboring countries would object to Japanese participation in Cambodia, this turned out not to be true. Public opinion of the operation in Cambodia was very favorable, and as the Japanese people obtain more experience in peacekeeping, public support for an expanded role in PKOs may grow. A review of the current law is scheduled in the summer of

1995. One issue that remains to be resolved is the variance between Japanese law and the UN definition of self-defense.

13. Peacemaking

One participant was highly critical of the peacemaking process in the former Yugoslavia and felt that it set a grave precedent by allowing frontiers to be changed by force. It was noted that while impartiality is important in humanitarian efforts, it is not always correct in mediation efforts where principles of international law and norms must be maintained. Moreover, negotiated solutions should not involve finding a solution that is equidistant from the parties' positions.

The importance of balancing both "carrots" and "sticks" in negotiations with the parties was also highlighted. One participant mentioned that too much reliance on threats only ends up in further escalation. The need to develop the range and use of positive incentives which could provide "leverage" was stressed by several speakers.

The UN's capacity for peacemaking remains underdeveloped, although the Office of the Secretary-General, if it had the resources and desire to do so, is empowered to take strong initiatives.

14. Preventive Action

Although it was not the subject of the Colloquium, several speakers highlighted the need for better preventive action and the cost-effectiveness of such action. Yugoslavia was mentioned as a lost opportunity in terms of preventive diplomacy. As one participant stated: "If ever a crisis were predictable. . ."

One speaker questioned whether the UN was using the correct methodology and asked whether it was possible to establish peace in an intrastate conflict using the usual means. He called for a deeper analysis of the causes of conflict and proposed that preventive action should not only encompass preventive diplomacy, but should also be expanded to include a wide array of methods, including economic solutions. Although acknowledging that structural reform of the UN was difficult, he pointed out the need for such reform and the possibility of including the Bretton Woods institutions in preventive action. In this context, he posed a series of questions: Are the policies of the Security Council based on a sober analysis of the causes of intrastate conflicts? Is it possible to establish peace in intrastate conflicts using the usual means? Should we not be tackling the underlying causes? What kind of leverage can be used? How is it possible to use these resources before conflicts arise? Is the present structure suited to peacemaking? The problems in Algeria, for example, if carefully analyzed, might be amenable to such preventive action through debt relief or other assistance which would help the country find a way out of its impasse.

PROPOSALS FOR THE FUTURE

The following list represents the various suggestions made directly or indirectly by participants for improving the UN response to peace and security threats. These do not reflect unanimous agreement of the participants, but, rather, the range of ideas proposed:

- Any decision to move from peacekeeping to peace enforcement needs to be done consciously and in an ordered way. The Security Council may wish to reconsider the wisdom of mixing Chapter VII measures with Chapter VI operations.
- The short and long-term consequences of using force need to be clearly considered and weighed in each situation, especially the loss of impartiality at all levels.
- Peacekeeping operations should strive to maintain consent of the parties and be seen to be acting impartially.

- The Security Council should strive to be non-selective in its approach to problems in order to maintain international norms, as well as its legitimacy.
- The tendency to rely too heavily on "sticks" should be addressed by a more creative search for "carrots" as a source of leverage.
- Peacekeeping and peacemaking need to be better integrated.
- To assist the implementation of peacekeeping operations, the Security Council should give more attention to making its mandates clear and achievable and to specifying the legal basis for mandates. In this regard, it might be helpful for the Security Council to make a practice of consulting the Office of Legal Affairs on such resolutions. Regular consultation would also assist coordination between Member States and the Secretariat and avoid differences in interpretation.
- The conclusion of Status of Force Agreements should be a precondition for the Security Council to approve an operation. This would ensure the consent and cooperation of all of the parties, thus maximizing the chances of success of the operation.
- Stronger action by the international community is needed to reinforce the safety of UN personnel through a new international legal instrument. Careful consideration is needed, however, of the complex issues related to the criminalization of parties.
- Additional resources are needed at UN Headquarters to provide a proper infrastructure for peacekeeping. Member States should take the necessary measures to ensure that such resources are available.
- Member States should pay their arrearages. A new means of sanctioning those who do not pay arrearages should be devised if Member States continue to refuse to meet their obligation in this regard.
- The UN must have integrated units to avoid difficulty with command structures.
- Procurement problems need to be solved; multiple bidding is too cumbersome.
- A better system for contingency planning is needed for both the

Security Council and the Department of Peacekeeping Operations. Resources should be earmarked before decisions are made.

- Integrated task forces for each peacekeeping operation would assist decision-making and coordination. Such task forces will require additional resources at Headquarters.
- The Special Representative of the Secretary-General needs to be given greater discretion in decision-making.
- Member States need to work with the Special Representative of the Secretary-General to support or direct him. In addition, the Secretariat should increase its consultations with Member States, in particular with countries contributing to a particular operation.
- Member States need to examine more closely what to do in situations of decaying consent, examining questions such as what forms of leverage might be used for bringing a recalcitrant party back into the process.
- Experts should be recruited to assist the security coordinator in furthering the safety of UN personnel in the field. The Secretariat should inform the Security Council as to whether the security arrangements are satisfactory.
- Although actions can and should be taken to minimize casualties among peacekeepers and other UN personnel in the field, Member States need to realize and help their constituencies understand that a commitment to maintaining international peace and security will necessarily exact a toll.
- The traditional peacekeeping philosophy should be adapted to intrastate problems and become "people-centric."
- Related to this, civilian units are needed which can develop a closer link to the population (including through a consultative mechanism), which have a sizeable human rights component and which, in general, are more oriented toward peacebuilding.
- Peacekeepers need to exercise cultural sensitivity and a certain humbleness. When possible, the parties should be involved in the decision-making to inculcate habits of the democratic process and

conciliation.

- Transitional governments may provide a useful intermediary confidence-building step in some post-conflict situations.
- Peace accords in situations of internal conflict should contain provisions for the structural change of the society to address grievances in issues such as human rights, etc.
- Elections should not be added on to peace agreements to solve problems but need to be integrated into an overall strategy for reconciliation and constructive state building.
- Better supervision of the civilian areas is needed by the Department of Peacekeeping Operations.
- Training is needed for both military and civilian peacekeepers, including in the area of human rights.
- Economic rehabilitation can be an important positive incentive and should be an important part of post-conflict peacebuilding.
- A new use of the Trusteeship Council, which does not have colonial overtones, may be one approach to dealing with "failed states."
- Humanitarian assistance should not be used as a substitute for other kinds of effective action which would resolve the source of the humanitarian problems. The UN needs to be careful not to allow humanitarian actions to become an excuse for overall inaction.
- The Security Council may need to consider further how the UN should respond to forced population movements.
- The UN system needs a more effective means of meeting the needs of internally displaced persons.
- The UN needs to strengthen the capacity of its agencies to handle emergency situations quickly.
- Better mechanisms and structures are needed for early preventive action which tackles the causes of the underlying problems.
- Preventive deployment and "robust peacekeeping" may both be promising developments, but further testing of these new approaches is needed through their judicious use.
- The conditions under which sanctions are effective need to be

reviewed.

- The UN should conduct a review of all of its instruments as part of its 50th Anniversary.

It was noted that despite the new problems facing peacekeeping, UNPKOs will remain central to the conduct of international relations because states prefer to act multilaterally. It was also noted that the situation in the former Yugoslavia could have been worse if individual states had been involved.

In summary, changes are needed at both the macro and micro levels in order to promote peaceful change. It is only by careful examination of the new challenges facing the international community and by a thorough review of its current instruments and their practice, as well as through creative consideration of new methods of approaching such problems, that we can hope to improve our approach to the maintenance of international peace and security.

CONTRIBUTORS

Professor Georges Abi-Saab is Professor of International Law at the Graduate Institute of International Studies. A member of the Institute of International Law, he is the author of numerous books and articles, including *International Crises and the Role of Law: The United Nations Operation in the Congo 1960-1964*, and editor of *The Concept of International Organization*. Professor Abi-Saab is also judge on the United Nations International Criminal Tribunal for the Former Yugoslavia.

Mr. Yasushi Akashi was appointed by United Nations Secretary-General Boutros Boutros-Ghali as Special Representative for the former Yugoslavia, and Chief of Mission of the United Nations Protection Force (UNPROFOR), effective from 3 January 1994. Previously, Mr. Akashi had served as the Special Representative of the Secretary-General for Cambodia from 9 January 1992 to 25 September 1993. Prior to his appointment as Special Representative to Cambodia, Mr. Akashi served as Under-Secretary-General for Disarmament Affairs from March 1987. He had also served as Under-Secretary-General for Public Information from 14 May 1979. Before joining the United Nations organization, he was Ambassador at the Permanent Mission of Japan to the United Nations.

Dr. Mats Berdal is a graduate in International Relations from the London School of Economics and Political Science and Oxford University. He is a Research Fellow at the International Institute for Strategic Studies in London where he has specialized in the study of UN peacekeeping operations and, more generally, the use of force in international relations after the Cold War. His publications include *Whither UN Peacekeeping?* (Adelphi Paper 281, 1993).

Mr. Maurice Bertrand is former senior counsellor to the French Cour des Comptes and former member of the UN Joint Inspection Unit (1968-1985). He is the author of numerous articles and books on international relations, including "La Stratégie suicidaire de l'Occident" (Bruylant, Bruxelles 1993), and "L'ONU" (La découverte, Paris 1994).

Dr. Ronald Dreyer was a member of the electoral component of UNAVEM II in Angola and ONUSAL in El Salvador. Presently, he is Deputy Director of the Electoral Division of ONUMOZ in Mozambique. He is a Research Fellow at the Graduate Institute of International Studies and author of *Namibia and Southern Africa. Regional Dynamics of Decolonization (1945-1990).*

Professor Victor-Yves Ghebali is Professor of International Organization at the Graduate Institute of International Studies. His fields of specialization are the CSCE process and the UN system. He has written extensively on both topics.

Mr. Serge Lalande is a lawyer and doctoral candidate at the Graduate Institute of International Studies. He is a former research assistant with the Peacekeeping Training Program at UNITAR in New York and has published on the Special Committee of Peacekeeping Operations.

Mr. Elie Marcuse works in the Division of Political Affairs of NATO and is currently one of NATO's top experts on Multilateral and Regional

Affairs, with special expertise in the new European security architecture. Mr. Marcuse was formerly the chief reporter for *l'Express*, responsible for security issues such as European defence and disarmament.

Mr. Sergio Vieira De Mello is a career official of the United Nations. He served UNHCR in various functions, including Director of External Relations, and was Senior Political Advisor of the UN Interim Force in Lebanon (UNIFIL). He was Delegate of the Special Representative of the Secretary-General in Bosnia-Herzegovina before becoming Head of Civil Affairs of UNPROFOR.

Mrs. Sadako Ogata has been United Nations High Commissioner for Refugees since 1991. Prior to her nomination, she was Dean of the Faculty of Foreign Studies at Sophia University in Tokyo. Mrs. Ogata was the representative of Japan on the United Nations Commission on Human Rights as well as delegate of Japan to various sessions of the General Assembly. She also served as chairman of the Executive Board of UNICEF. She has been a member of the Trilateral Commission since 1984 and served on many government advisory councils and on the boards of academic associations and foundations.

Mr. Hisashi Owada is Ambassador, Permanent Representative of Japan to the United Nations, New York. Prior to that appointment, he held numerous positions in the foreign service of Japan, including Ambassador of Japan to the OECD in Paris, Vice-Minister for Foreign Affairs and Adviser to the Minister for Foreign Affairs. Concurrent with his professional activities in foreign affairs, Mr. Owada has been engaged in academic activities, teaching International Law and Organization at Tokyo University as well as being a Visiting Professor at Harvard University (1972-82 and 1989), and is currently adjunct Professor of International Law at Columbia University (1994-) and Inge Rennert Distinguished Visiting Professor at New York University (1994-), and has authored numerous writings on international affairs.

Dr. Connie Peck is currently Coordinator of the UNITAR-IPA Fellowship Programme in Peacemaking and Preventive Diplomacy. During 1992, she was a Special Consultant to the Australian Foreign Minister studying what was needed to strengthen the UN's capacity for peacemaking and preventive diplomacy. Dr. Peck was Chairperson of the La Trobe University Institute for Peace Research and is the author of four books and over 50 publications on conflict resolution, the UN and a number of other topics.

Professor Steven Ratner is Assistant Professor at the University of Texas School of Law, where he teaches international law and related subjects. From 1986-1993, he served in the Office of the Legal Adviser at the United States Department of State, including as legal adviser to the U.S. delegation to the Cambodia peace talks. From 1992-1993, he was an International Affairs Fellow of the Council on Foreign Relations.

Mr. Ralph Zacklin is Director and Deputy to the Under-Secretary-General, Office of the Legal Counsel of the United Nations. He has served with the United Nations since 1973 where he is responsible for the legal aspects of peacekeeping and good office missions. Prior to joining the United Nations, he served as Director of the International Law Programme of the Carnegie Endowment for International Peace. He has taught at several institutions, and has published several books and articles in the fields of international law and international organizations.

LIST OF INVITED PARTICIPANTS

Curt GASTEYGER	Professor, GIIS, Director, Programme for Strategic and International Security Studies
Vera GOWLLAND	Professor, GIIS
Paul GROSSRIEDER	Deputy Director of Operations, International Committee of the Red Cross
Hansrudolf HOFFMANN	Acting Director, Division of International Organizations, Federal Department of Foreign Affairs, Switzerland
Tatsuro KUNUGI	Professor, International Christian University, Japan, and Former Special Representative of the UN Secretary General for Humanitarian Assistance to Cambodia
Sverre LODGAARD	Director, United Nations Institute for Disarmament Research, Geneva
Toshiki MOGAMI	Professor, International Christian University, Director, Peace Research Institute, Japan

Vladimir PETROVSKY	Director General, United Nations, Geneva
Adam ROBERTS	Montague Burton Professor of International Relations, Oxford University
Bruno SIMMA	Professor, University of Munich
Marie-Claude SMOUTS	Director of Research, National Center of Scientific Research, Paris
Alexander SWOBODA	Director, GIIS
Anton THALMANN	Head, UN and International Organizations Division, Federal Department of Foreign Affairs, Switzerland
Theodor WINKLER	Representative of the Chief of the General Staff for Politico-Military Affairs, Federal Military Department, Switzerland